Quantitative Business Planning Techniques

Quantitative Business Planning Techniques

James P. Fourre

American Management Association, Inc.

About the Author

JAMES P. FOURRE is Vice-President of Marketing and Planning with Pillsbury Management Systems Co. in Minneapolis. He was previously Systems Manager on the 1108 computer with the Univac Division of Sperry Rand Corporation. His background of experience includes responsibility for linear programming on the large-scale Univac 1107 and 1108 computers and work with linear programming and other mathematical programs during his previous association with Philco Corporation. Mr. Fourre is a respected author in the field of computer techniques.

This book has been distributed without charge to AMA members enrolled in the Manufacturing Division.

International standard book number: 0–8144–2141–5
Library of Congress catalog card number: 75–128011

Foreword

WITHIN the next ten years every reader of this book will have an opportunity to use a computer in solving some problem. I have chosen four fairly popular, but challenging, techniques that can be applied to the computer: network scheduling and resource allocation, computer simulation of modern business problems, inventory control systems, and linear programming. In each case we will develop a general working knowledge of the technique, do several sample problems, and then propose a practical system for implementing the program on a computer. We will cover some of the programming considerations, and discuss the hardware required to implement the system.

In the area of implementation we will concentrate most heavily on the human interface to the computer or, more appropriately, to the problem. We will discover that each of us is able to communicate with the aid of simple command languages that we can learn in *just* a short time. It is also important to learn how much computer hardware is required to solve certain types of problems. Unfortunately, many off-the-shelf packages that are available are not adequate. In some cases the system requirements for a job have been underestimated, because the program designers have been caught up in their own advertising and think the computer is "smarter" than it really is. If there is anything more costly than a computer to solve our problems, it is a computer that will not solve our problems. It will cost more to add on the necessary equipment afterward than it

5

would have if the correct system had been purchased in the beginning. We must be certain, therefore, that the system we buy will handle our problem, and that we shall not find ourselves hopelessly committed to an expensive system that requires more and more expenditures for additional equipment.

The way to avoid this predicament is to know our system and the system requirements. Unfortunately most literature available to businessmen today is written on a fairly technical level, which makes it difficult to gain enough of an understanding of the techniques and their application to properly analyze the systems. I have therefore approached each of these techniques with the intention of familiarizing the reader with what it cannot do as well as with what it can do and with what is *not* needed in the way of equipment as well as what *is* needed. The manager is the man who identifies the business problem that exists and who best understands what the specific job requirements for that problem are. The manager, then, should also understand the techniques that are available to solve that problem.

JAMES P. FOURRE

Table of Contents

SECTION ONE

Network Scheduling
and Resource Allocation

This section deals with a new technique in business planning. It involves the incorporation of the concept of resource allocation with the concept of network scheduling, and offers a very realistic and practical approach to solving business planning problems. In addition, two extensions will be added to the technique: money, or cash flow, will be treated as a critical resource in the network; and the concept of resource smoothing will be applied to the network. A new use for scheduling networks will also be introduced. In the past, they have been used mainly for determining a schedule from a given set of ordered activities. We will develop a justification and a method for using the network as a planning aid. In addition, we will discuss in some detail the design of a system that will enable us to implement our technique on an electronic computer.

1

Network Scheduling

A NETWORK consists of an ordered set of activities (arcs) and events (nodes). Nodes are connected by arcs, and in the network schedule no event is complete until all the activities required for it are complete. Activities are related to time, and events are related to the completion or start of an activity. Two important events in the network are the start (the "source"), and the finish (the "sink"). The start event has no event preceding it, and the finish event has no event succeeding it. Between these two events there are a series of unique paths, each of which consists of a collection of arcs and nodes that connect the start event to the finish event. Each path through the network is unique in that it contains at least one activity that is different from an activity in another path.

This network is supposed to reflect and act as a model of something real, such as a product. Using a model enables us to obtain information about the product, without having to incur the cost of actually building it. We must be aware, however, that the answers obtained from a model are only as accurate as the model itself.

The Network

Exhibit 1.1 illustrates the simplest of all networks; it consists of two events and one activity. The two events are "start job," denoted by S, and

EXHIBIT I.I

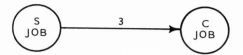

"complete job," denoted by C. The activity, the effort that went into completing the job, took three units of time to complete, and is indicated by the arrow between the two events. Normally, in the network, the activity arrow flows from left to right.

Exhibit 1.2 shows a more detailed network, having intermediate events and activities that follow the start-job event and lead to the complete-job event. We will assume that a particular part or top assembly consists of three unique parts, A, B, and C, which must be tooled before being assembled, and that part A requires 4 weeks of tooling, part B requires 5 weeks, and part C requires 2 weeks. These intervals of time can be seen on the activity arrows between the start and complete events for each part.

Notice that there are arrows leading from the "start of job" event to each of the events that starts the tooling on parts A, B, and C. These activities are shown at zero (0) time. Activities with zero time are developed to handle situations where multiple activities are to start after a single event is reached. They are called "dummy activities" and represent no actual change to the network. The same type of dummy activities are included leading into the start-assembly event of the final part. It would be possible to eliminate the latter dummy activities by simply eliminating the completion events for each of the parts and allowing the tooling activities to lead directly into the start-assembly event.

EXHIBIT I.2

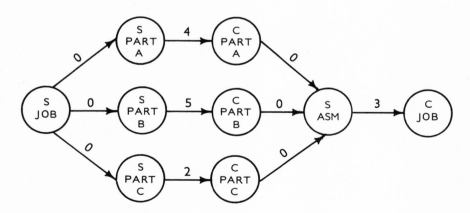

12

This leads us to a unique rule in network scheduling—no event can occur until all activities preceding the event are complete. In this specific case the start-assembly event cannot occur until parts A, B, and C have all completed the tooling phase. This means that the part that takes the longest to tool will determine the amount of time that elapses before the start of the next assembling activity. The total job time illustrated in Exhibit 1.2 is 8 weeks, because the start-assembly event cannot take place until part B is tooled, which takes 5 weeks, and it takes 3 more weeks to complete the assembly activity.

The Critical Path

At this point a simple network scheduling technique called CPM, the Critical Path Method, will be described. The total job time for a given network is equal to the sum of the activity times along the longest path through that network. As we indicated earlier, a network has many paths. To identify each path in a large network can be an almost impossible computational task; however, we can count the paths by starting at the finish and working backward.

In Exhibit 1.3, we start at event number 11 and place a zero (0) below it, showing that there are zero paths from event 11 to the finish. Working backward to event 9, we place a 1 below it, indicating that there is one path from event 9 to the finish, event 11. We do the same at event 10. At event 7 we place a 2 below it indicating that there are two paths from 7 to the finish. We see that there are 2 paths to the finish from event 6 along the path to event 7, (6–7–9–11 and 6–7–10–11), and 1 path to the

EXHIBIT 1.3

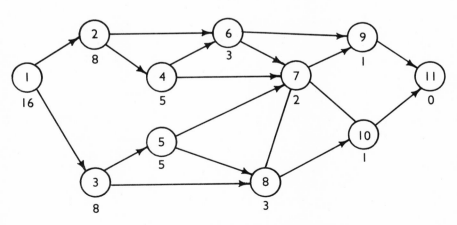

finish along the path from 6 to 9, (6–9–11). We enter the total number of paths, 3, below event 6.

We can determine the exact number of paths that there are from a given event to the finish by adding the number of paths from each of the succeeding events to the finish. Continuing to work backward in Exhibit 1.3 to the start event, we find that there are exactly 16 unique paths through this network. There are usually more paths through a network than there are activities; in this case there are 11 activities and 16 paths. In larger networks this difference reaches almost geometric proportions. To determine the longest path through the network we need only sum up the activity times along each path. The longest path gives the total job time, and this path is called the *critical path* in the network.

Keep in mind that the networks are established on the basis of estimates prior to starting the actual job. The network itself, and the time estimates for the activities, will determine the output from the analysis. If the network or the activity times are in error, then the total job time will be in error. The best solution to the problem of faulty estimates is to allow the people who will actually be working on the activity to do the time estimating.

A Sample Schedule

It is now possible to set up a sample business problem using this network scheduling technique. Let's assume that a manufacturer is developing an end product that will necessitate procuring three unique parts, which, when they arrive, will require special machining on each of two unique pieces of equipment. After the machining, there will be several phases of hand assembly, and finally the product will be painted. In developing the network schedule for this job, the first step is to list the unique activities and estimate the time for their duration.

1. Procure part A = 3 weeks.
2. Procure part B = 2 weeks.
3. Procure part C = 4 weeks.
4. Cut part A on machine M = 2 weeks.
5. Cut part B on machine M = 1 week.
6. Cut part C on machine M = 2 weeks.
7. Cut part A on machine L = 2 weeks.
8. Cut part B on machine L = 2 weeks.
9. Assemble parts A and B = 2 weeks.
10. Assemble part C with A and B = 2 weeks.
11. Paint final product = 1 week.

These 11 activities constitute all the activities required to complete the product for the delivery.

The next step is to set up a network that orders the activities. Exhibit 1.4 is the network for this job. It has been developed to allow all possible overlap of activities. Following the top path along the network, we start and complete event 1, which is procure part A. We then start event 4, machine part A on machine M, which is completed three weeks later. Next we start event 7, which is cut part A on machine L. Notice that this event cannot actually start until event 8, complete cutting part B on machine L, is completed. This is because we cannot start using machine L on part A until it is free from cutting part B. The network continues in this fashion until we reach event 11, paint final product.

Now we can determine the total job time, which, we recall, is the longest path through the network. The easiest way to determine this path is to start from the beginning of the network, at time 0, and work out into the network, developing the completion time for each event. For example, there are two paths from the start of the job to event S7. The longest path is along the top of the network and is six weeks in duration. The other path is through the middle of the network, from event 2 to 8 and up to 7, and is only five weeks in duration. Six weeks, then, is the earliest time that we can start cutting part A on machine L. By doing this with all the events in our network, we can develop a table of event times as follows.

Event	Weeks	Event	Weeks
S1	0	C6	10
C1	3	S7	6
S2	0	C7	8
C2	2	S8	2
S3	0	C8	5
C3	4	S9	8
S4	3	C9	10
C4	6	S10	10
S5	6	C10	12
C5	7	S11	12
S6	8	C11	13

The table shows that C11 occurs at 13 weeks. The critical path through the network is therefore 13 weeks in duration.

The Earliest Completion and Latest Allowable Start Dates

Every event in a network has two dates associated with it: the earliest completion date and the latest allowable start date. The earliest comple-

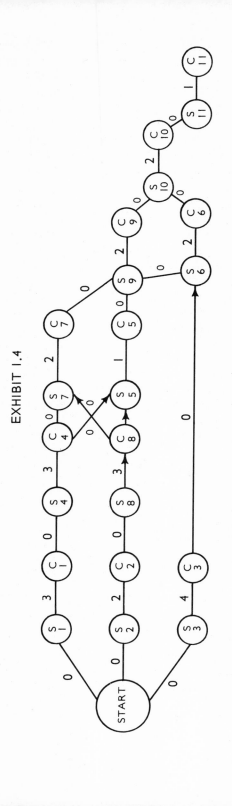

EXHIBIT 1.4

tion date (ECD) is equal to the longest path *from the start* of the network to the event in question. The latest start date is equal to the longest path from the event *to the end* of the network, and specifies the latest date on which the activity can start and not delay the finish date of the network. It should be clear that the time from any event along the critical path to the finish is the remaining time on the total job. If the event were to slip or to occur late for some reason, the total job would slip by that amount of time. Along the critical path, then, the latest start date for a given event is the total job time minus the remaining time along the critical path from that event to the finish.

For example, if the total job time is 13 weeks and some event on the critical path is 4 weeks from the finish, the latest allowable start date (LAS) is 9 weeks. This means that the activity should start at the ninth week. If the event starts later, the job will be delayed. For events off the critical path, the LAS date is more complex. This date is equal to the time along the critical path minus the time along the longest path from the event to the finish. For example, let's assume that the final network event is to occur at 13 weeks. The event in question has two paths from itself to the finish; one path is 4 weeks and the other is 5 weeks in duration. The LAS date then is $13 - 5 = 8$ weeks. We must start this activity at the eighth week or we can not get to the finish event in 5 more weeks, or in a total of 13 weeks.

The critical path gives us additional information about the events in the network. Along the critical path, the ECD and the LAS are equal. This can be shown by describing the contradiction that would occur if they were not. Let's assume that the total job time is 13 weeks, and that the longest path from a given event to the finish is 3 weeks; therefore, the LAS is $13 - 3 = 10$ weeks. Let's further assume that the ECD is less than the LAS, say, 9 weeks. This means that the total time along this specific path from the start, through the event in question, to the finish is 3 weeks plus 9 weeks, or 12 weeks in duration. The event cannot be on the critical path, because the critical path is 13 weeks long, not 12. This leads us to the conclusion that no event whose ECD is different from its LAS can be on the critical path, or conversely, any event on the critical path must have an ECD equal to its LAS.

Slack in the Network

We have recognized that certain events off the critical path do have different dates for an ECD and an LAS. The difference between these two dates is called the "float" or "slack." Physically, it corresponds to the amount of cushion we have at that event, or the amount of time that we can delay the start of an activity without delaying the total program. This slack will become an extremely important factor in resource allocation. For the time being, it should be of obvious value from the standpoint of its enabling us to determine which activities have slack, so that we can free resources from those activities and use them in activities on the critical path. This will, hopefully, shorten the path which in turn will shorten the total job time.

Advantages of the Technique

There are other valuable assets to the network technique. It can be used to determine how much the critical path needs to be shortened before it becomes noncritical and some other path becomes critical. This knowledge will help us avoid wasteful overtime, or the commitment of extra resources to an activity that is no longer on the critical path and will no longer affect the total job time. Other scheduling techniques do not offer this insight. The network technique offers an additional advantage in that it is a dynamic scheduling tool from the standpoint that once the network is developed, it need not be redeveloped with each schedule slip or gain that occurs over the course of the schedule. Once the network of the job is actually completed, we need only mark off each event when it is actually completed and, then, move out through the network recording the expected completion dates of the succeeding events.

The original schedule dates, as they were computed before the job started, can also be recorded near the event circles. We can use the difference between the original schedule date and the current expected completion date to determine how much slack has occurred in the schedule. If we desire, we may choose to fix the completion date of the job and use that as a reference for computing LAS dates for each unit in the network. The difference between this date and the ECD then becomes the slack at that unit on a fixed schedule. A negative difference would tell us that the unit is that many weeks behind a fixed schedule.

Probability Distributions and PERT

The PERT technique is merely an extension of CPM. All the concepts employed in CPM are employed in PERT, along with one basic extension. In CPM there is a single estimate of time for the duration of each activity. This estimate amounts to a best guess on the part of a man who is knowledgeable about the activity. In PERT this time estimate is extended into a distribution of times. Specifically, it requires three time estimates: a minimum time, an average time, and a maximum time. These three times are weighted in PERT on a 1–4–1 basis so that the average time gets four times the frequency of the minimum and maximum times. In the system this becomes a continuous frequency distribution on the basis of the three.

The distribution can be skewed left or right or be normal. The system uses all the distributions along the critical path and assumes that they add up to a normal distribution over the total path. This becomes a probability distribution, where we can say that the probability of completing the total job in some specific time will be given by the distribution. This is all true, of course, except that the individual numbers for each activity were guesses, which are no better than a single guess. To say, then, that the probability of finishing the total job by some time is equal to .3 (for example) is misleading. If somehow we were able to determine the exact distribution for each activity, which is of course impossible, we might find that the probability of finishing on time is .2. What is the maximum time for an activity? For any guess that one person makes, someone else can always say that one week longer is also realistic.

Not only is the probability misleading, therefore, it is also a useless number in most cases. What good is it to know that an event will occur at a certain time with a certain probability? The man who is concerned with the figure knows that it is an estimate in the first place. To add a probability factor tells him nothing. In most cases, then, it is much better to make a single best guess.

2

Resource Allocation

Rᴇsᴏᴜʀᴄᴇs are machines, people, materials, and other items that are needed to make a finished product. Their total cost equals the cost of the product. A major drawback of most network scheduling techniques, including PERT and CPM, is that the models they employ are unrealistic in this area; there is no provision for resources. They simply assume that resources will be available when required for an activity. In the real world, however, each activity competes with other activities for the available, limited resources.

When a job is under way, and resources become unavailable for one reason or another, schedule slips are inevitable. In fact, resource problems are the primary cause of schedule slippage. Frequently, for example, the same resource is scheduled for use on two different activities at the same time.

It is important, then, to explore ways of incorporating the resource-allocation concept into the network scheduling technique. One approach is to assume that on-time completion of network activities depends upon the availability of critical resources. Total resources are regarded as a pool that changes dynamically with the passage of time through the network.

An event cannot be started unless the required resources are available in the pool. If they are available, the pool is depleted by the required amount, which is then assigned to the activity, and when the activity is completed, the resources are reassigned to the pool. Activities in the network are now not only ordered in time, they are tied to the availability of the required resource.

Assigning the Resources

At this point we can develop a simple method of implementing this technique. Our problem is similar to our earlier one; a final product is the result of making several component parts. There are four parts that must receive special machining on three unique pieces of machinery. Let us also assume that there are two skilled operators, each of whom can run two of the three machines. However, only one of the three machines can be run by both operators. This should give us a good test of how the technique works and how resource availability can affect the schedule.

The table that follows shows the machines M1, M2, and M3; the operators 01 and 02; and which pieces of equipment each man can operate.

Machine	Operator	Parts
M1	01	A, B, C, D
M2	01 and 02	B, C, D
M3	02	A, C, D

All the parts, and which pieces of equipment each part is to be machined on, are listed in the right-hand column of the table. There is no particular order in which the parts are to be machined, any part can be machined before another. However, each part must be machined on the given pieces of equipment in a certain order. Part A must be machined on M1 before M3. Part B must be machined on M1 before M2. Part C must be machined on M2 before M3, and on M3 before M1. Part D must be machined on M1, then on M2, and then on M3. Some of the problem constraints can be set up in the network itself, while others, such as resources, will have to be handled dynamically in the technique.

Scheduling the Activities

The first step is to set up a table, Exhibit 2.1, of the activities and the required resources for the job. The left-hand column identifies the individual activities, and the right-hand column indicates the resources required for each specific activity. For example, activity number 2, Machine part A on M3, requires two limited resources, machine M3 and operator

EXHIBIT 2.1

Activity	Resources
1. Machine part A on M1	2 weeks M1 and 2 weeks 01
2. Machine part A on M3	3 weeks M3 and 3 weeks 02
3. Machine part B on M1	2 weeks M1 and 2 weeks 01
4. Machine part B on M2	2 weeks M2 and 2 weeks 01 or 02
5. Machine part C on M1	1 week M1 and 1 week 01
6. Machine part C on M2	2 weeks M2 and 2 weeks 01 or 02
7. Machine part C on M3	1 week M3 and 1 week 02
8. Machine part D on M1	1 week M1 and 1 week 01
9. Machine part D on M2	2 weeks M2 and 2 weeks 01 or 02
10. Machine part D on M3	2 weeks M3 and 2 weeks 02
11. Assemble parts A and B	1 week
12. Assemble parts C and D	1 week
13. Final assembly	1 week

02, for three weeks each. Activity number 6, Machine part C on M2, requires two weeks of machine M2 and two weeks of either operator 01 or 02. In this case, either operator will be satisfactory in that both can operate machine M2. In the resource technique we have two basic constraints for each activity: the availability of the required resources, and the completion of the required preceding activities. In this situation, for example, activity 9 cannot be completed, even though the required resources are available, because activity 8 must be completed first. These requirements can be pinned down by developing the scheduling network as illustrated in Exhibit 2.2.

The network shows the start (S) and the completion (C) of each of the numbered activities that correspond to the entries in Exhibit 2.1. In a CPM analysis of the network, the total job time equals the longest path through the network, seven weeks. When we incorporate resource allocation into our schedule, we cannot assume that all activities are independent of one another. For example, activities 1 and 8 cannot occur simultaneously, since they both require the same resource, machine M1. The resources are limited and will affect the schedule on this particular network.

Developing an Event-Oriented System

Refer again to the list of 13 activities in Exhibit 2.1. For the technique that we are developing, we are interested in an event-oriented system rather than an activity-oriented system like the one we used in CPM. In that system, each activity was defined by two events, "start activity" and

22

EXHIBIT 2.2

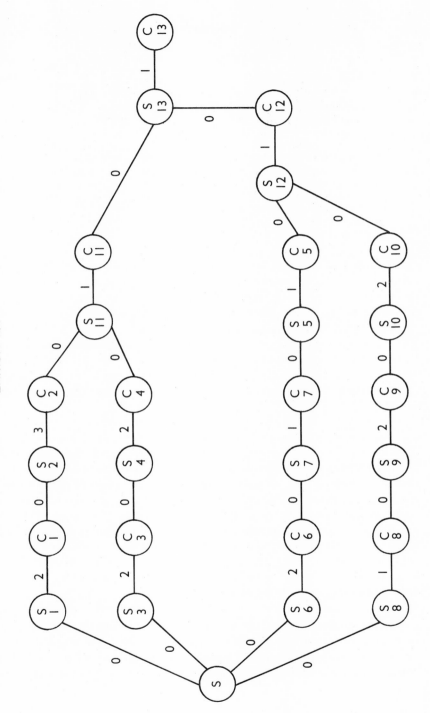

"complete activity." Normally in the resource allocation technique, the complete activity event for one activity becomes the start for the next activity. This need not, however, be the case. We can add dummy activities with zero time when necessary; however, this leads to additional computations and space requirements, and it should be avoided where possible. For our event-oriented system, we will arbitrarily relabel each activity according to the table that follows:

Old Activity	New Activity
1	1–2
2	2–3
3	4–5
4	5–6
5	9–10
6	7–8
7	8–9
8	11–12
9	12–13
10	13–14
11	15–16
12	17–18
13	19–20
*14	3–15
*15	6–15
*16	10–17
*17	14–17
*18	16–19
*19	18–19

If we drew a new network of events, with event 1 as the start of an activity and event 2 as both the completion of that activity and the start of another activity, we would have a network which would reflect the same story as the network in Exhibit 2.2. In some places, however, we would avoid dummy variables such as the one between complete activity 1 and start activity 2. On the other hand, we cannot avoid dummy variables where two events lead into one single event. The reason for this will become clear as we use the technique. These dummy variables, or dummy activities, are identified with an asterisk (*).

The set of events that constitute the activities for this job forms a continuous network; there are no "dead end" events in the middle of the network. Every event within the network has at least one activity leading into it and at least one activity leading out of it. The exceptions to this, of course, are the start and finish events. This can also be shown in the number scheme used for the new activities. With the exceptions of events 1 and 20, all other events have a preceding and succeeding event.

The objective of the technique is to develop a procedure which is as mechanical as possible so that it can be easily implemented on a digital computer. One is immediately drawn to a rectangular system with activities along the ordinate and time along the horizontal. With this scheme, we can use rectangular-array storage statements common to the FORTRAN program language. The implementation of our technique on a computer will be developed in Chapter 4. For now let's be concerned mainly with how the technique works.

Scheduling the Resources

The problem is laid out in tabular form as shown in Exhibit 2.3. The rectangular system is used, placing activities along the horizontal in weeks, with each box representing one week. The columns of information entered on the extreme left of the table contain key control information about the various activities. Reading from the left, column 1 is the "from" event for each activity and column 2 is the "to" event. The third column identifies a resource and the fourth column gives the quantity of that resource that is required in terms of weeks. The next two columns give the same information about another kind of resource. If we read across the first row from the left, we find from event 1 to event 2 that the resource M1 is required in the quantity of two weeks, and the resource O1 is required in the quantity of two weeks.

Notice that all the new activities are listed here in a certain order from top to bottom, with the starting activities in the top rows of the table. Activity 1–2 is a starting activity, because there is no activity that precedes it; there is no activity in the list that has a 1 in column two. On the other hand, activity 13–14 is not a starting activity, because 12–13 precedes it.

As we enter each activity into the table, we move down in the list to the next activity to see whether it qualifies as a starting activity. We continue to scan the list, working down to the end. Once it is complete, we delete all activities in the list that have been entered into the table. We then start to scan again, only now we are working with a reduced list of activities. We pick from this list the next set of starting activities placing them into the next available rows in the table. We continue in this fashion until all activities have been moved from the list to the table in an order that is approximately the same as the order of their occurrence in time.

This does not mean that an activity in the list will always occur before every activity below it in the list. However, it will insure that blocks of

EXHIBIT 2.3

FROM	TO	RESOURCE	QUANTITY	RESOURCE	QUANTITY	TIME (WEEKS) 1–15
1	2	M1	2	O1	2	bar weeks 1–3
4	5	M1	2	O1	2	bar weeks 3–5
7	8	M2	2	O1 O2	2	bar weeks 1–3
11	12	M1	1	O1	1	bar weeks 4–5
2	3	M3	2	O2	3	bar weeks 3–6
5	6	M2	2	O1 O2	2	bar weeks 6–8
8	9	M3	1	O2	1	bar weeks 4–5
12	13	M2	2	O1 O2	2	bar weeks 8–10
3	15	0	0	0	0	marker week 3
6	15	0	0	0	0	marker week 8
9	10	M1	1	O1	1	bar weeks 7–8
13	14	M3	2	O2	2	bar weeks 10–12
15	16	–	1	–	–	bar weeks 7–8
10	17	0	0	0	0	marker week 8
14	17	0	0	0	0	marker week 12
16	19	0	0	0	0	marker week 11
17	18	–	1	–	–	bar weeks 12–13
18	19	0	0	0	0	marker week 13
19	20	0	1	0	0	bar weeks 13–14

Resource	Weeks with requirement (ticks)
M1	1 1 1 1 1 1 1 (weeks 1–7)
M2	1 1 (weeks 1–2), 1 1 1 1 (weeks 6–9)
M3	1 1 1 (weeks 3–5), 1 1 (weeks 11–12)
O1	1 1 1 1 1 1 1 1 1 (weeks 1–9)
O2	1 1 1 1 1 1 1 (weeks 1–7), 1 1 (weeks 11–12)

activities will occur before other blocks lower in the table, and that activities near the top will occur, on the whole, before activities near the bottom. This will help us insure the optimum allocation of resources. Notice that the dummy activities are also entered in the natural order in the table, and that zeros are entered for their resource requirements. Because these activities do not require any time within the schedule, they have no impact on the finish date.

In addition to the activity information in the left-hand columns, we have in the lower left-hand corner of the table a list of resource availabilities or the resource pool. This is used to identify the specific resources and to keep track of the quantity available at any given time in our schedule. For example, the first resource in the pool is the machine M1, which is available in the quantity of 1. The last resource in the pool is the operator 02, who is also available in the quantity of 1. Other resources can be added below these if required.

The scheduling technique is a relatively simple one. We commence scheduling activities from the top of the list and work down, because no activity is dependent upon an activity below it in the list. Scheduling an activity consists of meeting the following rules:

1. Within the same row as the activity, draw a bar equal in length to the largest resource requirement.
2. The bar should be as far to the left as possible.
3. The bar for any activity must be completely to the right of a bar from any preceding activity.
4. A bar can be drawn only through columns where resources are available in the pool.
5. When entering a bar into the chart, subtract the required resources from the pool during the interval of time covered by the bar.
6. At no time may the resources being used in a column exceed the total resources available.

Following these general rules will produce a feasible schedule whose end date will be shown by the end, or extreme right-hand, position of the bar that is farthest right on the chart. This will usually be somewhere in the lower right-hand corner of the chart. If all information is entered correctly during the scheduling, the total resources used in each week will be recorded in their corresponding column on the chart. The best way to explain the technique in detail is by specific example.

We start at the top of the list by entering a bar of two weeks' duration into row one of the chart. The two weeks represent the resource requirements: two weeks of both M1 and 01. This meets rule 1. The bar is pushed to the extreme left of the chart, thereby meeting rule 2. Rule 3 is automatically met, because there are no preceding activities. Rule 4 is met because this is the first activity scheduled and no resources have been used. Rule 5 is satisfied by entering the resources used into the resource rows in the lower part of the table. The specific rows are those labeled M1 and 01. Notice that, in columns one and two of these rows, ones are entered to indicate that the resources are in use during this period of two weeks. Rule 6 is met because the resources used do not exceed the quantity available.

We next schedule the second activity in row two. Notice that the activity is independent of the first and therefore could be scheduled during the same time interval of two weeks. This cannot be done, however, because the resources M1 and 01 are already in use. The activity must therefore be scheduled during weeks three and four, as shown by the bar in row two. Completing the rule requirements, we record in the resource rows M1 and 01 the fact that these resources are being used during that time interval. This is accomplished by adding ones in these rows at columns three and four. The chart now shows that this activity will be completed at the end of week four.

We continue by scheduling the next activity in the third row. This bar is entered at the extreme left, because it is not dependent upon the first two activities and because the required resources are available. The resources required are M2 and either 01 or 02. M2 is available, and therefore it is assigned to the activity by placing a one in columns one and two of the row labeled M2 in the resources. Either operator, 01 or 02, could be used; however, because operator 01 is already assigned, we must use operator 02.

The fourth activity is entered in row four, column five. This is as far to the left as the bar can be entered. The reason for this is not that the activity is dependent upon another activity, but that there are resource shortages. Notice that the resources used during the interval are assigned to the activity by entering ones in column five of rows M1 and 01 of the resource rows.

The fifth activity is scheduled by entering a bar into the chart on row five according to the rules. Rule 3 states that the bar must be completed to the right of any preceding dependent activity. In this case, activity 2–3 must be to the right of activity 1–2, because 1–2 must be completed before 2–3 can start, even though the required resources are available. We must therefore enter the activity in columns three, four, and five and also assign the resources being used to the appropriate resource rows. This process is continued in the chart until all activities have been scheduled.

Notice that a dummy variable is represented by a dot in the same column that the activity immediately preceding it finished in. Activity 3–15, which is a dummy, is preceded by 2–3, which finished in column five. A dot is therefore entered into column five. This dot is used later in scheduling activity 15–16, which must occur to the right of the preceding event that is farthest right on the chart—in this case, 6–15.

When all activities have been scheduled, we can determine the total job time. This is shown by the end of the bar at the farthest right on the chart—in this case, activity 19–20, which will be completed at the end of thirteen weeks. In the network (Exhibit 2.2) where resources were ignored, the schedule took seven weeks. This is almost twice as fast, seven weeks instead of thirteen, as our estimate incorporating resource allocation. We see that by using the resource allocation technique we get a much more realistic schedule.

The technique developed here is quite similar to other resource allocation techniques. There are some differences that make it a bit more cumbersome, but these were introduced to make the technique easy to implement on a computer. If we follow the six general rules and use the rectangular layout in the chart, the schedule becomes a simple repetitive technique that should be easy to understand.

There are two special cases that should be discussed here. Let's assume that an activity requires one type of resource for two weeks, another type of resource for one week, and a third type for one week. This is usually handled by breaking up the activity into two unique activities with each activity assigned the same quantity of resources. In this case the two-week resource can be broken up into two one-week resources and scheduled for two separate activities. The two remaining resource requirements can be assigned, one to the first activity, the other to the second. In this fashion, all resource requirements for each activity will be one week in duration. The second special case occurs when resources are available in multiple quantities. Let's assume that resources M1 and 01 are available in quantities greater than one. In this case, the total schedule might have been improved. Notice that this increased pool of resources would allow us to schedule both the first and second activities simultaneously. Activity 11–12 may also be scheduled two weeks earlier. This tells us that the availability of resources may affect the schedule in a number of ways. We will explore this further when we use the concept of a variable resource to meet a fixed schedule.

3

Extensions to the Technique

In THE preceding chapter, we developed a straightforward, simple approach to resource allocation. We are now in a position to introduce extensions that will make the technique extremely practical for other planning problems. Specifically, we will cover the areas of resource smoothing and money, or cash flow, as a critical resource, and resource allocation as a planning aid. The techniques, as applied to these areas, are relatively new concepts. They may need changing in certain areas to fit specific applications.

Resource smoothing is a technique that is employed to keep the resources used as close to a fixed level as possible. The level itself does not necessarily have to be a specific quantity, but can be determined from the job requirements. It may, for instance, be the average resources used per week taken over the whole job, it may be some fixed value, or we may wish to minimize the variance from week to week.

The technique used here will be to minimize the variance on a single resource only. The technique could be expanded to include several critical resources; however, this would be an unusual requirement. Normally, several critical resources are used on a job, but only one requires smoothing. Manpower is usually a good example. It is not good planning to have too many men around one week, none the next week, and then several the week after that. It would be better to smooth out the manpower requirements over the three weeks, provided that we don't affect the schedule. There may even be some latitude in slipping the schedule to avoid situations with large variances in the specific resource. We will find as we develop the technique that resource smoothing utilizes the concept of "float" or "slack" in the network to determine whether an activity can be scheduled earlier or later without affecting the schedule.

A Sample Problem

The chart shown in Exhibit 3.1 will serve as an example. Following the rules developed in the preceding chapter, activities are entered along the left-hand side, starting with activity 1–2 and going down to the last entry, activity 7–9. In this example, only a single resource is used. The technique that we shall employ, however, can be expanded to use several resources. The quantity of the resource M needed for each activity is entered in the fourth column in terms of the number of weeks it is required.

EXHIBIT 3.1

FROM	TO	RESOURCE	QUANTITY	TIME (WEEKS)
1	2	M	2	
1	3	M	3	
1	4	M	2	
2	5	M	0	
2	6	M	3	
3	5	M	4	
3	4	M	0	
4	8	M	2	
5	7	M	4	
6	7	M	0	
6	9	M	2	
8	7	M	0	
8	9	M	2	
7	9	M	3	
Total		M		3 3 2 3 3 3 3 1 1 1 1 1 1 1

In this schedule, we assume that there is an unlimited amount of resource M available to perform the job, but we want to smooth out the amount used over the duration of the job. If we add up the resources in each column and enter the sum in the row labeled "total," we get a picture of the resource commitment at each period during the total job. This in itself is a handy piece of information, provided that the individual estimates are fairly reliable. The information can be used for planning ahead to get the necessary resources in time to meet the schedule.

The solid bars on the chart (Exhibit 3.1) show the actual schedule for the job; the total job time is 14 weeks. The dotted lines are drawn in after all the solid lines are completed and a total schedule is available. These dotted lines represent the "float" or "slack" of the activity. We recall that the float or slack means the amount of play or the amount of delay that can occur at an event without affecting the total schedule. Recall also that slack occurs only at events that are off the critical path. Events on the critical path have no slack; they must begin immediately after the completion of the preceding event so as not to delay the total schedule. In this example, activities 1–3, 3–5, 5–7, and 7–9 are on the critical path. All other activities, with the exception of the dummy activities, have dotted lines to indicate slack. The dotted line shows that activity 1–2 can be slipped out to the right, up to week 8, without affecting the total schedule.

Determination of Slack in the Schedule

How are these dotted lines computed? We start from the bottom of the list and ask ourselves whether the last activity in the list can be pushed out to the right without affecting the schedule. In this case the answer is no. If we push activity 7–9 to the right, we will lengthen the schedule; therefore, that activity has no slack. The next activity (working up) is 8–9. We can push it out to the right as far as week 14 without affecting the schedule, so we enter the dotted lines. We can do this because pushing an activity to the right will cause no delay in the activities above it, only in those below it. The chart is arranged so that all activities above the one in question either are unrelated to it or precede it. Therefore, we need to check only the activities below the one in question to see whether any succeed it. If they do, we can push the completion of the activity up to the start of its succeeding activity.

Working up the list, we come to activity 8–7, which is a dummy. Here we move the data out as far to the right as possible, to the end of week 11, because activity 7–9 must start no later later than the 11th week; therefore,

8–7 must be completed no later than the 11th week. Next on the list is activity 6–9, which can be moved all the way to the 14th week, because activity 9 is not the start of any other activity. We continue this process until we reach the top of the list. The chart now shows us where we have slack in the system.

By actually moving the solid lines around on activities that have dotted lines, we can change the resource load from week to week without affecting the total resources required on the job. We can now attempt to smooth the resource requirements, which in our case are heavy in the early stages, over the entire job. We must keep in mind, however, that by pushing slack activities out to the right we eliminate their slack and thereby make them a critical activity. By definition, any event with zero slack is a critical event. The more critical events there are in a network, the more of a chance there will be for a schedule slip.

The Smoothing Technique

To begin the actual smoothing process, we start to reschedule the activities at the bottom and work up. The basic approach will be to reschedule an activity in such a manner that the variance in availability of resources is at a minimum. We can get a relative measure of the variance for the total job by computing the sum of the squares of all the resources. The sum of the squares without rescheduling can be taken from the resource row at the bottom of Exhibit 3.1:

$$S = 3^2 + 3^2 + 2^2 + 3^2 + 3^2 + 3^2 + 3^2 + 1^2 + 1^2 + 1^2 + 1^2 + 1^2 + 1^2 + 1^2$$

The objective of the technique is to minimize the sum of the squares, which we will call S. The basic rule for the minimization is to pick the lowest activity on the list and reschedule it to a time when S is a minimum. In case of ties, choose a time farthest to the right. Continue this procedure on the next activity up the list, rescheduling it to a time when S is a minimum. While rescheduling each activity, keep in mind that it cannot be scheduled to the right of, or in the same time position as, any of its successors—it must be completely to the left of its successors.

In Exhibit 3.2, a total rescheduling has been accomplished. Notice in the row labeled "Total" that the smoothing is almost perfect. There is no possible way to get resource variance any lower. We start off with one unit of resource in the first week and then step up to two units in all succeeding weeks to the completion of the job. The resource-smoothing technique is practical in situations where resources would lie idle during

EXHIBIT 3.2

FROM	TO	RESOURCE	QUANTITY	TIME (WEEKS)
				1 2 3 4 5 6 7 8 9 10 11 12 13 14 15 16 17 18 19 20
1	2	M	2	▬▬ (weeks 1–3)
1	3	M	3	▬▬▬ (weeks 1–4)
1	4	M	2	▬▬ (weeks 3–5)
2	5	M	0	● (week 8)
2	6	M	3	▬▬▬ (weeks 7–10)
3	5	M	4	▬▬▬▬ (weeks 4–9)
3	4	M	0	● (week 8)
4	8	M	2	▬▬ (weeks 9–12)
5	7	M	4	▬▬▬▬ (weeks 7–12)
6	7	M	0	● (week 13)
6	9	M	2	▬▬ (weeks 11–13)
8	7	M	0	● (week 13)
8	9	M	2	▬▬ (weeks 14–16)
7	9	M	3	▬▬▬ (weeks 13–16)
Total		M		1 2 2 2 2 2 2 2 2 2 2 2 2 2 2

slack periods and still accrue cost. In such a situation, it would be desirable to reduce cost by reducing the idle resources. Manpower is an excellent example of a resource that it is highly desirable to smooth.

Money as a Resource

A second interesting extension of the resource allocation technique is the concept of cash flow or money as a critical resource. It is not unrealistic to assume that many activities within a job are dependent upon the availability of money. In other words, they cannot be started or completed until certain funds are made available. This is, in many cases, more realistic than assuming that a certain fixed level of resource is available in a given period. Money is probably the commodity that actually makes the resource available.

Cash output. There are two basic factors that must be considered in the cash flow technique: the input and the output of money. The output is a relatively simple concept to handle. We assume that each activity in the list has money as one of its critical resources. It is expressed and handled, however, somewhat differently from other resource requirements for the activity. The entry is made following the activity name and adjacent to the label given to cash. It represents the total amount of cash required for the duration of the activity rather than a weekly or a per period amount. The implication is that this total amount of cash must be made available before the activity can start.

Cash input. On the other side of the ledger we must consider cash input; where the cash that will provide for the activity requirements is coming from. A list of several potential sources of cash for a job follows:

1. Accounts Receivable
   a. Cash made available during the course of the job from sources and activities completely independent of the job itself.
   b. Cash made available during the course of the job from sources and activities dependent on the job itself.
      (1) Cash made available from resale of resources no longer needed.
      (2) Cash made available from the sale of certain intermediate products developed during the course of the job.
2. Bank and Investment Loans
   a. Cash made available through loans on an installment or time basis independent of the job itself.
   b. Cash made available through loans at certain key points during the job. These would normally come at the completion of certain key milestones that demonstrate satisfactory progress to the lending institutions.
3. Stocks and Bonds
   a. Cash made available from the sale of a new stock issue. This can be sold at varying times throughout the job or at certain key completion milestones during the job.
   b. Cash made available from the sale of bonds at certain key points during the job.
4. Initial Cash Authorization: Money authorized within the company and redirected to the project to be charged against it.
5. Cash Authorization from Customer
   a. Cash made available from the customer at initiation.
   b. Cash made available from the customer at the completion of certain key milestones in the job.

Each source of cash represents a unique variable and requires special handling in the cash flow algorithm. In developing the algorithm we have a choice: We can allow for a rigid inflow of cash, and determine the schedule according to its availability; or we can schedule activities without regard to the cash requirements (only recording them in their proper time frame) in order to finish as soon as possible, and use the results to determine the cash required at each unit of time during the job. We shall find each alternative to be valuable. If, for instance, time is not critical, but the inflow of money is, we can record the cash inflow as fixed and determine the schedule from there. If, on the other hand, we want to finish the job as soon as possible, we schedule the activities as soon as possible, without regard to cash, and determine from the result the required cash.

The basic approach to dealing with activities and resources in the cash flow technique is the same as that used in resource smoothing. However, we must expand those rules to include the cash flow rules. In developing the list of activities, we show the total cash required for each activity. This can be done by adding a pair of columns, one for the resource identification and the other for the amount in dollars, to cover the cash outflow.

To cover the inflow we need to employ two methods: one if cash inflow is job-dependent, another if cash inflow is job-independent. The job-dependent cash inflow is handled by adding unique activities to the list with a zero time requirement so that the activity will not add time to the total job. It will insure only that the cash inflow will not occur until its preceding dependent activity has been completed. The activity is similar to a dummy activity, except that it is used to introduce cash into the job at some ordered point in time. For example, let us assume that after the completion of activity 7–8, cash can be made available. We then create a dummy variable with zero time and label it activity 8–9, so that it will occur after 7–8. We enter for this activity the amount of dollars acquired at that point in a negative amount in the column for quantity of the money resource. The negative value quantifies the amount of the money resource that the particular activity consumes. For activities that actually use the money resource, we enter the amount as a positive quantity so that when we subtract that amount, we reduce the current cash available. However, when we subtract a negative quantity, we actually *increase* the total amount available.

The second method of introducing cash into the system is by job-independent events. These events and their cash amounts are entered in a special row near the bottom of the table. We enter each of them in the column at the point at which they are scheduled to occur. As the scheduling proceeds, elements from this row are added to the current cash-on-hand row to determine the total cash available from the independent sources. The total amount of cash inflow is given by the sum of the dependent and the independent sources.

The technique can best be illustrated with a more detailed example. Let's assume that we have a job that requires one resource that is in short supply, and that money itself is a critical resource. We will further assume that a maximum of 2 units of the resource is available at any time. The total cash requirements for the job are $137,000, and this figure is broken down into the individual activity requirements shown in Exhibit 3.3. To offset this cash outflow, it has been determined that $4,000 per week can be made available from independent sources within the company. A quick glance at the scheduling requirements shows that if this were the sole source of cash for the job, it would take 35 weeks to accumulate sufficient cash to finish the job. It is decided, therefore, to arrange for addi-

EXHIBIT 3.3

FROM	TO	RESOURCE	QUANTITY	RESOURCE	QUANTITY	TIME (WEEKS) 1–20
1	2	M	2	C	7	bar weeks 1–3
1	30	M	3	C	11	bar weeks 1–4
1	4	M	2	C	8	bar weeks 2–4
30	31	0	0	C	-12	• week 3
2	6	M	3	C	18	bar weeks 4–7
31	50	M	4	C	21	bar weeks 8–11
31	4	M	0	C	0	• week 3
4	8	M	2	C	9	bar weeks 5–7
50	51	0	0	C	-12	• week 12
51	70	M	4	C	27	bar weeks 12–15
6	71	M	0	C	0	• week 9
6	9	M	2	C	8	bar weeks 8–10
8	71	M	0	C	0	• week 8
8	9	M	2	C	11	bar weeks 15–18
70	71	0	0	C	-12	• week 16
71	9	M	3	C	17	bar weeks 15–18

	Week →	1	2	3	4	5	6	7	8	9	10	11	12	13	14	15	16	17	18	19	20
M 2		2	2	2	2	1	2	1	2	2	1	1	1	1	2	2	1	1	1		
C 4		4	4	4	4	4	4	4	4	4	4	4	4	4	4	4	4	4	4	4	4
C		20									20										
Total Cash Avail.		6	10	6	4	8	3	7	2	6	10	14	3	7	0	4	3	7	11		

tional sources of cash at intermediate points along the way. Two bank loans are scheduled as one source of additional cash. One $20,000 loan will be set up immediately, and another $20,000 is scheduled to be available after 8 weeks. This will supply an additional $40,000, but it is felt that this is still an insufficient amount of cash to produce the best schedule. As a final source of cash, it is decided to tie the inflow to the schedule itself by acquiring $12,000 cash at the completion of each of three key milestones, thus providing an additional $36,000 during the course of the job. These three sources represent the total cash inflow for the job.

Rules for Scheduling with Cash

The scheduling technique that will be employed is identical to the one employed in resource smoothing, except that we shall extend some of the rules to cover the cash flow problem. The following additional rules will be applied to the cash flow problem:

1. Schedule each activity as far to the left as possible where sufficient cash is available.
2. Subtract the quantity of cash required for the activity from the total cash available row. If this creates a negative amount, add the quantity back in and try to schedule it farther out to the right where more cash may be available.
3. To determine the cash available in any one period, add the cash from all dependent sources to the total cash available in the preceding period. The computation of the total cash available row can start in column one and then can be computed out to the right as far as is needed to schedule the early activities. When an activity is scheduled, its cost must be subtracted from each of the columns in the total cash available row as far out to the right as it has been computed.

We can now schedule the activities as shown in Exhibit 3.3. We begin by scheduling activity 1–2 into weeks 1 and 2, and subtracting the cash requirements of $7,000 from the total cash, $24,000, that is available at this time. This leaves $17,000 total cash available. We also add in the total of the other resource used, which is one each for weeks 1 and 2. This is entered in the row labeled M near the bottom of the table. We have now scheduled the first activity, after having found that sufficient resources were available, and we have deducted the resources from the pool.

Activity 1–30 is scheduled next and can be entered in weeks 1 through 3, because sufficient resources are available. The activity requires one unit of resource M for each of the three weeks; therefore, we add 1 to row M in columns one, two, and three. The activity requires $11,000 cash, which is also available in the pool; therefore, $11,000 is subtracted from the row labeled "total cash available." This leaves $6,000 in the pool at the end of the first week.

Next we schedule activity 1–4. We cannot schedule it in week 1, because there is neither enough money nor enough resource M. In week 2 an additional $4,000 becomes available, making a total of $10,000 in the pool. This is enough cash for the activity, but there is still not enough of resource M. Resource M is available in week 3, which is where we schedule the activity.

The next activity in the list can be scheduled any time after activity 1–30 is completed. Notice that the activity requires no resources. This is a dummy activity that is designed to introduce additional cash into the system. We schedule the activity as far to the left as possible and subtract the cash requirements for the activity from the pool. This necessitates updating the pool. We add the last period's cash available, $6,000, to the current period's cash inflow from independent sources, $4,000, which gives us a total of $10,000 at the beginning of period 4. When we subtract the negative quantity of cash contributed by activity 30–31, we actually increase the total cash available by $12,000, giving us a new total of $22,000. This figure is entered into column four of the cash available row.

We continue this scheduling process until all activities have been scheduled. In this case, the total job takes 18 weeks. Notice that if we had scheduled activity 31–50 before scheduling activity 2–6, the job would not have taken as long. Problems like this can be identified and slack in the system can be drawn out by rescheduling all activities in the list, starting at the bottom of the list as far to the right as possible. As we move an activity to the right its resource requirements are also shifted to the right, but interestingly, the cash requirements do not change to the right of the activity—only to the left.

As an example, assume that we move activity 2–6 as far to the right as possible. We can move it all the way up to activity 6–9, which can be moved out to week 18. This means that we can move 2–6 out to week 17. As we move it to the right, we add to the total cash available row the cost of the activity. This figure is added to the columns just vacated. For example, if we reschedule 2–6 to weeks 5, 6, and 7, which is equivalent to moving it right one week, we then add $18,000 to the cash row in column four. There will be no change in columns five, six, and seven. In other words, any activity can be rescheduled to the right without regard to the cash requirements.

By rescheduling in this fashion, activity 6–9 moves to weeks 17 and

18, activity 2–6 to weeks 12, 13, and 14, and activity 4–8 to weeks 10 and 11. Weeks 5 through 8 are completely open and one additional week of resource M is available in week 9. This permits us to move the first three activities to the right to fill these gaps, leaving weeks 1 through 5 completely vacant. We can now move the total job back five weeks without affecting the order of activities or the resource allocation, and we have a total job time of 14 weeks instead of 18 weeks. This demonstrates the value of rescheduling activities in order to remove a good portion of the system slack.

In most of the sample problems that we have dealt with in studying resource allocation, we have encountered situations where the available resources were fixed and the schedule was allowed to vary freely. As we proceeded through the tables and scheduled each activity, the only constraints were that sufficient resources be available and that any given activity was not scheduled to occur before all or any part of a preceding activity was completed. As far as the total job time was concerned, we allowed the chips to fall where they might. We have not yet considered a situation in which we allow the resources to vary and we fix a schedule that must be met.

Earlier in the chapter we developed a technique for smoothing out the resources employed over the total job. In the last example we only shifted slack activities around to smooth out the requirements over the interval; we did not reduce the number of resources required to complete the job. This will remain fixed in any of the problems we consider. The object of allowing the resources to vary is to determine whether the job can be completed according to a fixed schedule. In scheduling, it often happens that we wish to determine the required resources for completing a job in a certain amount of time. This is also useful in determining cash requirements in a job where money is a critical resource. The basic technique here is to allow resources to accumulate without restriction so that we get as short a schedule as possible. If the schedule beats the required completion date, we use the smoothing technique that we developed earlier in the chapter.

Resource Allocation as a Planning Aid

In addition to using resource allocation as a means of determining the total number of resources required for a job, we can use it as a planning aid in determining a possible optimum tradeoff between resources and schedule. The procedure is to initially select a minimum number of resources for the job. After an examination of the resulting schedule, a decision is made to change the resources and recompute the schedule. The results are reexamined, and the process is repeated until a satisfactory tradeoff is obtained. The technique requires a considerable computational effort that can be implemented only on a digital computer. We will explore this area in more detail in the next chapter, because the technique is an extremely valuable management tool for planning.

A related procedure that is also useful in the planning area is to develop a schedule around the minimum possible resources and, from the resulting table, develop strings of related activities. For example, in Exhibit 3.1 the first string includes activities 1–2, 2–5, 5–7, and 7–9. The second string is 1–3, 3–5, 5–7, and 7–9. By eliminating activities from the list when they have been included in all possible strings, we can insure that all the strings are computed. One approach is to build up trees of strings from the first activity to the last. This requires searching out each string through the list. Once this is done, the first activity in the list can be eliminated. The technique is repeated until all activities have been eliminated.

Associated with each string is a number that is computed by adding the quantity numbers for the required resources for each activity in that string. Once we have resolved all the strings and computed their number, we choose the string with the largest number. This string corresponds to the critical path in a pure network approach to the problem. We shall call this string the critical string in the resource approach. If the critical string equals the initial scheduled time for the job, no amount of additional resources will improve the schedule. If, however, the two times are not equal, additional resources applied at the right time will improve the schedule.

We can determine the time and the amount of additional resources by examining the critical string in the initial schedule. To start, check the second activity in the string to see whether it was delayed by a shortage of resources in the initial schedule. If so, the amount of required resources can be immediately determined. A check can be made of the initial schedule at each of the critical activities to determine whether any slack exists between the two connected activities. If there is slack, additional resources will eliminate it. An analysis of this kind can be extremely valuable and cost-saving. It will show what a minimum effort will produce, and exactly where and how many additional resources must be applied to get the best possible schedule without wasting resources.

4

Resource Allocation
Applied to the Computer

In THIS chapter we will discuss and develop a general systems design for a resource allocation package on a digital computer system, and examine both the hardware and the software required to implement the program. The design used here is not the only one that is feasible; the kind of hardware that is available may dictate a different design.

The first step in developing a systems design is to give a functional description of the package, telling what the package should do, what kinds of problems it will handle, and the sizes of those problems. It should pin down not only the general structure of the system, but also the description of the system that is to be implemented. Henceforth, when we refer to the system or to the package, we shall mean the program developed on the computer system that will perform the resource allocation function.

To start with, let's pin down what we want the package to do. The following is a numerical listing of the functional requirements of the package. The first requirement establishes that the system will, upon command, be able to execute the rest of the functions listed.

1. The system will accept basic systems commands contained in columns 1–6 on punch cards. Each command will direct the program to a

different area, depending upon the intent of the command. The commands will be interpretive; as soon as the program reads in the command and interprets it, it will cause the immediate execution of the command. The program will be expanded, or enhanced, by the addition of new commands to the system and to the program that executes the commands.

2. The package will read information about the job on an activity basis. It will recognize starting and completion events and information pertaining to resource requirements. If there are not any resource requirements for an activity, it will recognize a single entry that gives the time, or duration, of that activity. If the activity has resource restrictions, the system must differentiate between two types of critical resources. One type will be a cash resource, which, we recall, receives different handling than the other resource. All information pertaining to a single activity will be contained on one punch card in prespecified columns. As an alternative to punch cards, we may use a key data recorder, which enters information directly on magnetic tape. The package will store the information it reads onto the mass storage system, and the maximum number of activities handled will be 2,000.

3. The system will condense the activity information about the job into a more simplified form. This will include giving a numerical name to activities with an alphabetic name, and renumbering activities that have excessively large numerical names. An index will be created for resource identification. When external conventions, or names, are adopted to ease the human interface, but internal conventions can ease the memory and handling problem, these conventions will all be indexed. The internal conventions will remain within the program, and when an external inquiry is made about a certain activity or variable, the program will go through the indexing system to obtain the answer. In this way, all program inputs and outputs will be on the basis of the external names, but the program can operate using the internal conventions.

4. The system will read the activity information into the memory of the system and sort the information in order of occurrence. All activities that precede other activities will be entered at the top of the list, and all activities that succeed other activities will be lower in the list. During the sort, all resource information will be carried with the activities.

5. The system will read in, via punch card, parameter information controlling this particular run, and will set the specified parameters to the specified values. Each parameter setting will be contained on a single punch card supplied by the user. Such variables as the names of the two different resource types, the unit of time being used, and labels to be used on printouts are examples of parameters that can be entered by the user. The parameter names will be preentered into the system, and when a new

one is to be entered, it will be placed at the bottom of the list. Each parameter will have a number relative to the beginning of the parameter list as its storage location in the parameter storage area. If the parameter is the 24th parameter from the beginning, it will be assigned the 24th location in the parameter storage. If expansion is desired as a design proceeds, or even after it is completed, new parameters can easily be entered into the system.

6. The system will make a forward pass on the activity list and schedule all activities as far to the left as possible.

7. The program will print out the total schedule, as it currently exists in the computer, in a bar chart form. Activities will be listed on the vertical axis, and time will be displayed along the horizontal axis.

8. The program will smooth out the resource use on the resource named in the command.

9. The program will reschedule all activities in the list as far to the right as possible. The latest activity in the initial schedule will be used as the anchor activity on the right. This command should help eliminate slack in the schedule.

10. The program will shift all activities as far to the left as possible, updating all resource rows. This command will normally be used after the command 9 is used to shift the schedule to the beginning of the chart.

11. The program will determine the critical string within the list of activities, marking that string within the list.

12. The system will schedule the list of activities, giving resource priority to those activities marked as part of the critical string as a result of command 10. This command will help achieve a minimum-optimum schedule.

13. The system will compute the quantity of resources and the time when they are needed, to insure that there is no slack between two successive critical activities. This row will be printed out. The computation will occur on the basis of the current schedule within the computer. The command assumes that a critical string marking command has been previously executed.

14. The system will print out the current state of the cash row within the computer. This will allow for a separate examination of the cash flow situation.

15. The program will schedule all activities, allowing cash outflow to be computed and recorded in the cash row without affecting the schedule. The other scheduling commands will treat the cash row as a critical resource and allow the scheduling of activities only when sufficient cash is available. In this command, only a recording of the cash requirements takes place. This allows for a separate analysis of the exact cash outflow

required at any given time during the schedule. The command will be extremely helpful as a planning aid in determining the amount of cash that is required for the total job. Later, as the system is enhanced, the prices of certain known standard resources, or the cost of a given activity, can be prerecorded in the system. This information will not have to be reentered each time the activity is entered; therefore, the activity will automatically trigger a reference to the standard cost file.

16. The program will store all the activities in the current job onto mass storage. Later, this information can be retrieved and processing can continue, as though the information were just read in from punch cards.

17. Certain activities that are currently in the file can be deleted upon command. Another command will add new activities to the file.

18. The total system can be dumped on magnetic tape in its current state, thereby recording a copy of the system as it exists at any given time. If there is a system failure, we need only drop back to this tape in order to renew the processing, instead of starting computation from the beginning.

19. The system will read a specified magnetic tape, and treat the data on the tape as though it were the result of a previous dump on magnetic tape. Computation will begin where a previous day's computation ended, just before the dump was taken. In this fashion, it is possible to split up the running of the job over several days.

20. The system will print out the current list of critical activities marked by command 11. If these activities are currently scheduled, their schedule dates will be printed adjacent to the activities.

These are just a few of the basic functions, presented in our list as commands, that are required for the kind of scheduling system discussed in the preceding two chapters. Appropriate names are given to the commands, such as LOAD for the command described in item 2 on the list. These commands can be punched in columns 1–6 of a card; all other data, such as activities and resources, can be punched in columns 7–80. This arrangement will enable the basic control mechanism of the program to identify easily where one command ends and another begins. Data can be entered between command cards.

This basic structure provides for maximum flexibility in the package. The design's greatest value is the ease with which new commands can be added to expand the system. The design parallels that of a programming language, in that the user can program his own requirements with super-instructions or commands. To make the language complete, we need only add branching capabilities to the language. This can be done by uniquely numbering each command in the command string. We might, for example, designate columns 72–75, on command cards only, as "command label columns," where the user can punch in any unique label he desires. We then add an additional command which will cause the control portion of the program to go to the command with the specified label, if a certain specified condition is met. If it is not met, the control should proceed to the next command in the string. As the user begins to work and experiment with the system, he can add and delete commands as the need arises.

As we have already discussed, all data input will be on punch cards. Command information will be entered in columns 1–6 and data information will be entered on data cards in columns 7–80. Columns 72–80 of the command cards will be used for the command label. We can use either a numerical or alphanumeric label, depending upon the degree of sophistication we require. The activity name will be entered in columns 7–17 on the data cards. Remember that the activity name consists of two parts, each of which corresponds to an event in the network. In this instance, the two parts, or two events, are the starting event and the completion event.

Columns 18–80, a total of 62 columns, will be used for entering the resources required for the activity. Arbitrarily assigning 10 columns per resource, we have space for six resource entries. In case there is a need for more entries, we will establish the convention that if anything is punched in column 80, the system will accept the next card as being part of the same activity. If we follow this procedure, we punch the name of one resource and the quantity required in columns 18–27, another resource and the required quantity, in columns 28–37, and so on. The first completely blank resource field will indicate an end to the required resources for the activity specified on the card. Other types of data input cards can be uniquely identified by preceding the card with a special command to alert the system to its presence. There will be a requirement for special labels, and output formats, and certain parameters, all of which will be entered in the card form.

The system should have the capability to receive command, activity, and resource data from sources other than cards. One method of implementing this is by adding the information from magnetic tape; the other is by adding it from the computer keyboard. There are two principal reasons for using magnetic tape. One is that many systems use magnetic tape as the principal input and output device; the other is that the system may not have a punch card device. In a magnetic tape system, all printing is done in an offline mode. Keyboards, on the other hand, are connected directly to magnetic tape. On occasion, it may be necessary to run the entire system from the computer keyboard, entering add and delete information into the system to update an old job in the files. In instances when a quick run is desired, in order to make some small changes in a job that currently exists in the files, it is desirable and much more efficient to operate the system directly online from the computer keyboard, bypassing cards entirely. These two options should be a part of the system.

We have already discussed several forms of output from the system. Most of this output was to a high-speed printer. We decided to make a rectangular display of the activity on the vertical, and display the time on the horizontal in the form of a bar chart, as in the Gantt technique. In addition, we provided for other types of output, including cash flow charts, critical string printouts, and punch card output for the dump program. When the user decides to do a restart dump, the card will contain required information pertaining to the format on the magnetic tape on which the system was dumped.

In addition to this, it may be desirable to display certain scheduling information on a cathode-ray tube, possibly in the form of bar charts. However, this would require a substantial addition to the program in order to give it a more conversational flavor. We must also provide for some output to the computer console printer. As you probably know, this is a rather slow device; therefore, it is desirable to minimize the amount of information that is printed on it.

The program and the data structure for this system are fairly simple and straightforward. To begin with, the program will be composed of two basic parts. One part is the command interrogation and control segment; the other consists of the basic commands themselves. The first part reads command information into the system, and searches a list of known system commands to see whether there is a match. If a match is found, the control program transfers control to the segment of the program that executes the command. If no match is found, the control segment prints out an error message and stops.

Later, when the user develops a greater familiarity with the system and his own requirements, he may desire to build up super-commands. These super-commands, called system MACROs, are made up of basic system commands, and are placed in the system's library. Whenever the control segment encounters a command that does not match anything in the basic command list, it searches the system library to see whether the command is a MACRO. If it is, then immediately following it in the library will be the basic commands which are to replace the MACRO. Once this is done, the control segment goes back into the control stream and starts interpreting the new commands.

The second part consists of the system commands which execute the various functions. These are written and checked out as independent segments of code or programs, and are normally called subroutines. They usually reside on some intermediate storage device, and are "called" or loaded into the main storage by the control segment, which, if it is not too large, will permanently reside in the main storage area. On the other hand, if the working storage requirements are fairly sizable, it is better to allow other command segments of the program to overlay the control segment, and thereby save on main storage requirements. When a command has been executed, the program will reload the control segment into main storage from the intermediate mass storage device. The basic idea is to structure the program so that it resides entirely in a mass storage device. During the actual running of the program, only the portion that is currently needed to execute a command will reside in main storage. This permits a maximum amount of main storage to be made available for the program data needed at any given time.

It is necessary to determine which part of the program will be stored on the intermediate mass storage device, and which part will be stored in the main memory. Main storage has the fastest access time; therefore, those parts of the program that are needed most frequently will be assigned to that area. Here, then, we will assign space for a table, similar to the tables we have used previously, except that there will be only two columns for the scheduling area. The basic scheduling commands will place dates in these columns, instead of drawing lines as we did. A "from" date and a "to" date will accomplish the same thing as a line drawn through the appropriate weeks in the table, and will cut down space requirements in main storage.

In main storage we will need as many rows as there are activities and as many columns as there are resources, plus four. Two of these additional columns will be used for the activity names—one for the starting event name and the other for the completing event name. These names will be internal system numerical names that will be equivalent to the numerical position of each event when it was read into the system from the original list. This same space will be used for finding and marking the critical string within the list.

We also need space to record the flow of both resources and cash on a time basis, as we did in the charts. This information cannot be kept in two columns; we need as many rows as there are resources and as many columns as there are weeks in the schedule. In addition to this, we need space for certain dynamic control parameters that will be required on a frequent basis. Other commands, such as those for loading and sorting, will need some working storage. The space that is normally used for scheduling can be used for those procedures on a temporary basis during the execution of the command.

The intermediate mass storage will be used to keep such data as card images of the initial problem as it was originally loaded. Some of the activities may have alphabetical names that must be kept in the exact image. An index, relating internal numerical activity names to external names, must also be kept here. This can be merely a numerically ordered list of the external event names. An exact map or image of the main storage schedule, a copy of the sorted chronological list of activities, a list and numerical ordering of the external names of resources, space for the system library, and a working area for the scheduling commands must also be kept in the intermediate storage. With the exception of a few basic control parameters, this accounts for the storage requirements.

This leads us to an examination of the specific requirements for the size of the storage. The main storage should contain about 32,000 words, which will be divided almost equally between data storage and the program. Of the 16,000 words used for the program, about 5,000 will be used by the executive or monitor program which is supplied by the manufacturer to control the job flow. The other 11,000 words will be used for the resource allocation program.

The mass storage requirements are substantially larger. The requirements will be approximately 500,000 words, of which a minimum of 200,000 words will be set aside for the resource program, and a minimum of 300,000 words for the data. If the amount of storage becomes insufficient, the initial and sorted activity lists can be kept on magnetic tape. This will release about 100,000 words of storage if it is a large problem.

The entire program will be written and developed in the FORTRAN programming language. There are a number of reasons for this decision. In the first place, FORTRAN is about the easiest language available. In the second place, FORTRAN is by far the most popular programming language and there are, therefore, many more experienced personnel available to operate such a program. In the third place, because of its relative simplicity, programming goes about five to ten times faster in FORTRAN than it does in so-called machine languages, and program debugging is about ten times faster. A program written in FORTRAN is also far easier to maintain and upgrade.

In addition, more computer systems have a FORTRAN compiler than any other compiler. FORTRAN also provides the user with a greater chance of compatibility than does any other computer system, compiler, or machine manufacturer. The problem of compatibility is one that has been plaguing the industry since 1955. First, program translators were tried. When they failed, some of the leading computer manufacturers offered what they called a compatible line of hardware—this also failed to solve the problem. I believe that the problem will ultimately be solved by a high-level compiler similar to FORTRAN.

There are other languages, such as COBOL and ALGOL, that offer some of the advantages of FORTRAN. Both are more sophisticated than FORTRAN, but because of this, they are more complicated and difficult to learn, and it is easier to make mistakes using them.

Probably the most insignificant decision to be made in developing the system is the choice of hardware, yet this is the area that receives the most attention. With few exceptions, price alone should be the major criterion for making this decision—provided, of course, that each prospective manufacturer of hardware has the identical system parts, so that we end up comparing apples and apples. The speed of the equipment will probably not be important, because the chances are better than 50–50 that the running time for any given job will be almost the same in two competitive systems.

The most important question to ask about the hardware is what software is available with it. It is here, and here alone, that the user will find his own interface with the system. He will not interface with the circuits of the machine, with the outlet on the wall, or with the core memory. His interface will be with the system software such as the monitor, or control program, and the compilers.

If the resource allocation program that we have proposed here is implemented, the interface will be at an even higher level than FORTRAN. It will be possible to have an interface where super-MACROs cause the computer to calculate values that pertain specifically to a company-related problem or application. In the past, the computer user has too often inherited a new company problem—the computer itself—instead of solving the company problem for which the computer was purchased.

There are six basic criteria for the hardware needed to implement the kind of system that we have discussed:

1. The main storage should have at least 32,000 locations, and each location should have at least 32 bits. Access time to this memory should be less than 10 microseconds.
2. No more than 6,000 words of the main storage locations should be used by the manufacturer's executive or monitor program.
3. The system should have a drum, disc, or other mass storage random access device. The capacity of the device should be at least 1 million words, and on the average, the access time to the device should be less than 100 milliseconds.
4. The system should have a standard 80-column card reader of any speed.

5. The system should have at least two magnetic tape units of any speed.
6. The system should have a high-speed printer that prints lines at a speed of 80 lines per minute, or more.

If a manufacturer can meet these criteria, and his price is lower than the price of any other manufacturer, his system is worthy of serious consideration. A 600 card-per-minute reader is not more desirable than a 100 card-per-minute reader, unless our requirement is to read continuously all day—in which case it will be necessary to employ a considerable force of keypunchers. We should not be overly impressed by the speed of the main storage either, since its speed is seldom a factor in determining total system throughput. The drum or disc memory device, however, may be a factor if the programmer is careless in developing his program. If, however, he takes into consideration the device's characteristics he can develop the program in such a way that he can offset the device's disadvantage relative to another manufacturer's device that appears to have an advantage.

This concludes our description of the basic hardware and software requirements that must be met to implement the resource allocation system. As the user becomes more familiar with the design and the system, he can make additions to it to fit his specific needs. The key to the design is to leave considerable room for expansion and change. He will find, as the system becomes debugged and relatively easy to use, that "outputs" from the computer will begin to creep into management reports. Such a system will allow the management of the company to better plan its resource and cash requirements, and to predict with a greater degree of accuracy the outcome of much of its work.

SECTION TWO

Simulation

This section of the book will deal with a relatively new technique called simulation. Until the introduction of the digital computer, simulation was an almost unknown science. The computer, because of its fantastic speed, made the technique practical, whereas previously, the amount of hand calculation had been beyond human ability. Simulation itself was an outgrowth of the computer. Sciences usually are developed out of a need or are an outgrowth of a breakthrough in the understanding of a particular physical or abstract phenomenon. With simulation this was not the case. It is not easy to define exactly what a simulation is. Many programs on digital computers today which have been labeled as simulators are as far from a good description of a simulator as any program could be.

Included in this section are a description of simulation and its relationship with other techniques, a discussion of the concept of time, which is crucial to simulation, and some of the simulation tools which are available on computers. These tools are basically compilers, not simulators themselves. In the last chapter, we will develop a computer system design.

5

The Simulation Technique

A SIMULATION is a model of a real physical phenomenon. The simulation of a process is a model which behaves in exactly the same fashion as the process itself. The model need not, however, be identical to the process in every detail, only in those details under study. As long as the simulation behaves like the real thing in the area in which we are interested, we can tolerate some differences. We will be studying computer models which are simulations of a real process. Normally, we attempt to simulate real things that vary dynamically; therefore, it is necessary that the simulation also vary dynamically.

According to the description presented here, a mathematical equation of an electrical circuit is not a simulation of the circuit. We will discuss the problem of what simulation is, and what it is not, in more detail later. This is an important question, because you will find that "simulation" is one of the most misused terms in the industry; there are many programs that are wrongly called simulations.

Exhibit 5.1 shows the relationship between a model and an actual process. In the real world, we usually find some kind of resources going into a process and a product coming out. We wish to learn more about the real thing by abstraction. We therefore develop a model that will behave as much like the process as possible. Into the model we feed data, and from

EXHIBIT 5.I

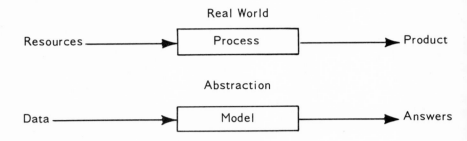

the model we get answers. The merit of the answers will depend entirely upon the merit of the model. There are, of course, tradeoffs. If we sacrifice some degree of realism in the model we may, if we are lucky, still retain a fair degree of accuracy in the answers. But this is always a gamble. It is important to note that a good model adds nothing to and detracts nothing from the real thing; like an equation, it only makes it easier to see what is there already. Too often in the past, the modeler's pencil has carried him away to the point where the model described more than the real thing.

Models for the Simulation

Many types of models can be considered in the area of simulation. Exhibit 5.2 illustrates the basic breakdown of the structure of the two general categories—abstract models and physical models. Abstract models are symbolic representations of such things as blueprints, equations, and computer simulations. Physical models, such as model buildings, thermostats, or analog computers, are characterized by their material or physical likeness to the real thing. It is interesting to note that a differential equation can be the same model as an analog computer, except that it qualifies as an abstract model instead of as a physical model.

In each category we have the subdivisions static and dynamic. A static model is one whose variables never change in time; a dynamic model's variables may change in time. In both of these categories, static and dynamic, we have the additional subdivisions linear and nonlinear. Linear models are characterized by those models whose variables are related by a constant for all values of the variables. Nonlinear models are characterized by those models whose variables are not related by a constant for all values of the variables. Linear programming is an example of an abstract, static,

EXHIBIT 5.2

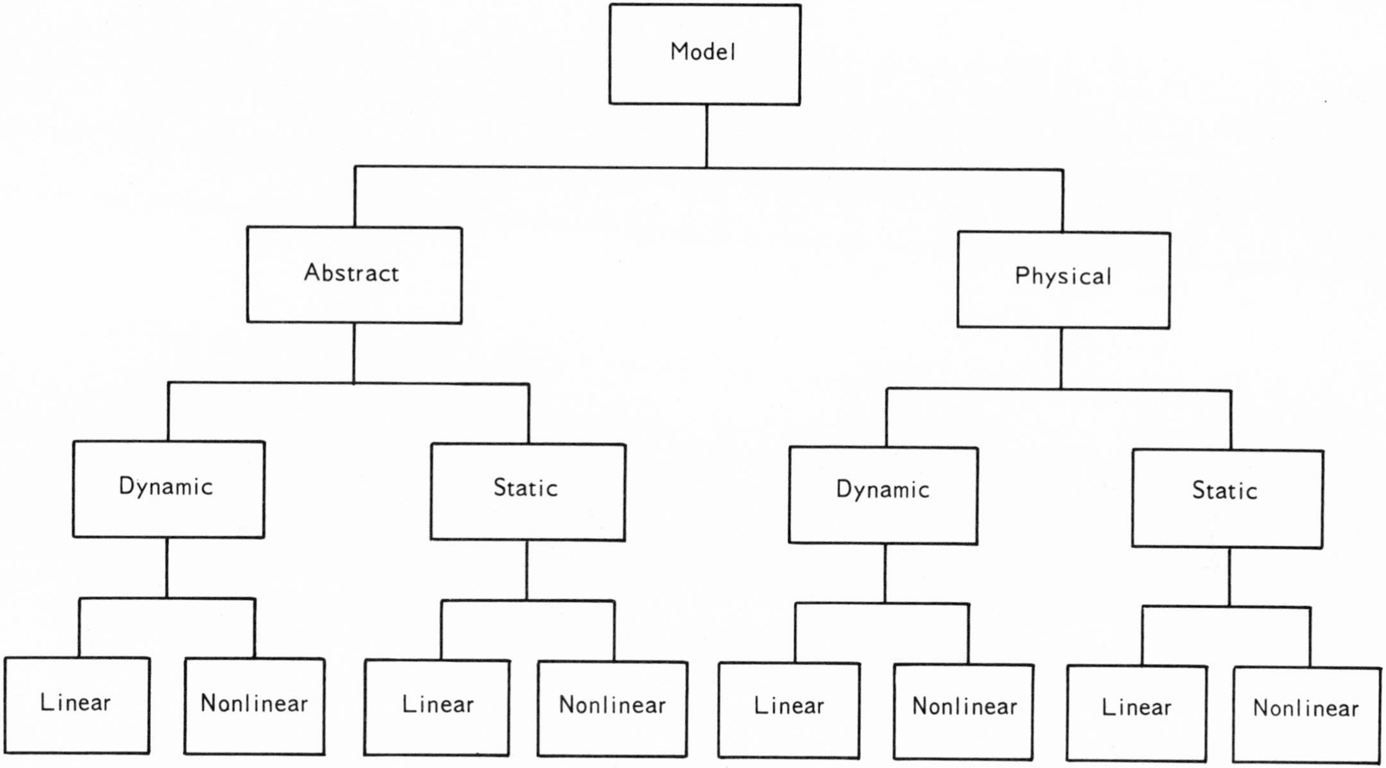

Model
Abstract
Physical
Dynamic
Static
Dynamic
Static
Linear
Nonlinear
Linear
Nonlinear
Linear
Nonlinear
Linear
Nonlinear

linear model. A differential equation of an electrical circuit is an abstract, dynamic model that can be either linear or nonlinear. A thermostat is an example of a physical, dynamic model. An analog computer's solution to the height of liquid in a tank where there is an inflow and an outflow is a physical dynamic model. In this case, the height of liquid in the tank is a variable which varies over time.

Static Versus Dynamic Models

We have thus far mentioned briefly the concept of static and dynamic. These two terms play an important part in simulation modeling. But they do apply differently in different modeling situations, so we must be extremely careful about how we use the terms. It is in this area that the most common violation of true simulation occurs, so let's elaborate the differences between static and dynamic. This is best accomplished by examining the real process rather than the model itself.

A static process, such as a network flow, is one in which the process variables never change in time. The flow in any leg of the network is dependent upon both the total flow into the network and its own relative resistance to the flow, but not, in theory, to time itself. The flow in the leg will tend to rise to a constant and remain there permanently. On the other hand, a process that has some capacitance, such as a system with several stages of vats or tanks, or an airport where customers are moved from one line to another in the various stages of processing, has dynamic characteristics. In the case of the tanks, the height of liquid in any tank is a function not only of input but also of time. In the case of the airport, the length of lines is also a function of both input and time; the length of any line will be determined by the number of people coming into the airport at a *given* time. It is important, then, to know not only the length of a line, but also the specific time at which that length occurs.

The quantity of inventory of a product in a company is a dynamic variable; it changes in time. We can visualize the level of inventory building up to a peak, and then, as time passes and demand takes its toll, gradually declining to a certain point at which a new order is placed. As time goes on inventory continues to decline until the resupply causes the level to rise sharply to its peak once again, where the cycle begins to repeat itself. These are just a few examples of static and dynamic processes. The concept is of interest, because simulation is, basically, the study of the behavior of various systems whose variables change in time as in a dynamic process.

Variables in the Process

Thus far we have given certain general definitions of simulation. It is now time to pin down a more detailed definition. To begin with, let us identify certain things that simulation is not. A simulation is neither a type of model that can be expressed analytically, by some form of equation, nor is it usually any type of static model. We shall find that most simulations are abstract, dynamic, nonlinear models; the model variables will change in time, and for the most part there will not be a constant relationship between any two variables. If there were, we could arrive at the value of one variable by an analytical approach from another variable. This leaves us with a technique which allows for the study of the relationship between process variables that cannot be related analytically.

We know that simulation is used to study processes. A process can be defined as a collection of interrelated variables, and a variable can be defined as an activity that produces a certain amount of output from a known amount of input at a given time. Looking into the heart of the process, we find many smaller interrelated processes.

Exhibit 5.3 shows a network effect within a process. The dots represent subprocesses or activities within the main process. The lines leading into the dots represent input to the activities and the lines leading out represent their output. The flow of input and the flow of output are considered to be variables, and the lines establish an interrelationship between the variables and the activities.

EXHIBIT 5.3

Process

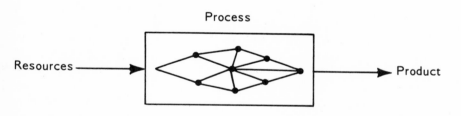

If there were an activity within the process which was not connected to another part of the process by lines or some type of interrelationship, then the activity would be totally unrelated to this process and could be considered independently. This implies, then, that every variable within a process *must* be interrelated with the other variables in the process; if it is not, it should be dropped from the model. The exhibit is, of course, an oversimplification of a process, but it should help in conveying an intuitive idea of what a process is.

In many models, the interrelationship between variables does not depend upon time or the order in which the activities occur. For example, suppose we are interested in shipping a given amount of product between two points by either of two methods: by airplane or by train. A third alternative, a portion by air and the remainder by train, also exists. We have, then, two variables which are interrelated. Their sum must be equal to a constant, but the order in which they occur and the time at which they occur is completely irrelevant and actually meaningless to the problem. In simulation, on the other hand, the order of their occurrence, the time of their occurrence, and their interrelationship with other variables are all important. According to our illustration, then, we can also define a simulation as a collection of process-related activities, organized to occur in a certain order in time.

A Sample Problem

It is important to note that the most perfect simulation of a subprocess is the subprocess itself. If it is economically feasible to use some of the real subprocesses in a total simulation, by all means do so—it will help make the model more authentic. For example, if we were going to simulate the subprocess of a queue caused by checking people out of a store, we could use a person as a checker for the simulation. He could be instructed to receive two types of people in his line, with each type requiring a different amount of processing time. The people would then be directed into either of two lines, depending upon their type. The object would be to have this checker simulate a part of a total system by deliberately creating a queue at himself.

During the simulation, we would not need real people moving through the queue; we would need only to tell the man periodically that people were entering his line. He could actually keep a written list showing how long his line was at any given time. We could also make up 100 pieces of paper with either a 1 or 2 written on them. If there was a 60–40 chance that any random person in the line would be a type 1 rather than a type 2, we would write "1" on 60 pieces of paper and "2" on the other 40 pieces.

After one person had been processed and the checker was ready to service the next person, he would draw, at random, one of the slips of paper from a box. He would actually wait the amount of time required to service the type of person he had drawn. At the end of that time, he would instruct the person who was handling the next line that one more person was going to enter that line, and then subtract one from his own list.

This is a simulation of a checkout station in a store. We actually used a person, and actually waited out the real amount of time for processing a single person in the line. If we had asked the checker how many people were in his queue at any given time, he could have looked at his list and given us the answer. We did not, on the other hand, perform any simulation of what the actual checkout consisted of; we were interested only in the length of the line.

If we examine the process more closely, we can see that it is possible to create this queue and simulate the activity with tools rather than with a person. We should be aware that there are many ways to simulate an activity; this is just one way to do it. We conclude by defining simulation as any means possible to recreate and duplicate the behavior of an activity within a real process. The ordered collection of these individual simulations becomes the simulation of the total process.

Simulation Versus Analytical Techniques

Comparing simulation techniques and analytical techniques is equivalent to comparing the real process with an analytical model of the process. To begin, let us examine what the real process is like. Is it like an equation? Is it like a computer program? The answer to both questions is no. Most processes can be compared roughly to a network with arcs and nodes; the network has directed arcs, where resources flow, and nodes that have capacitance (queues) to hold resources.

The best way to analyze a real process would be to jump onto a particle of resource and ride it through the process, observing where it went and how long it was held up at the various nodes. We could then record this information, go back to the beginning, and ride another particle through the process. On the second ride, we might find that we ended up taking a different route in a different amount of time. We could record the information about the second trip and start again, continuing this process several hundred times. We would eventually be able to compute certain averages and percentages, the values of which could be compared after each trip to see whether the values had settled down. When they did settle down, new trips through the process would add little.

At that point we would have learned a lot about the system; we would know, for instance, which were the major bottleneck areas and which were the least-problem areas. We might find that considerable traffic was queuing up at one node. That node might follow three other nodes, each of which performed the same task, and at which there were no queues. To add a fourth node at that stage would obviously be useless as a means of speeding up the total throughput. In an attempt to increase the total flow through the system, we might decide either to eliminate one of the three functions that were the same, or to duplicate the activity at the node where the queue was building up. Most good shop foremen and system operators learn the procedure for handling their job or process in a manner similar to this.

This technique is identical to simulation, except that in simulation we send simulated particles through the system rather than the real resources. We do, essentially, ride the simulated particle through the system, however, making observations as we go, just as we did above.

How does an equation of the process compare with this technique? There are actually no similarities; an equation is a static animal. Equations do not define the queue at a node at a given point in time or show the effect that a change in the queue at one node has on another node. They do not explain the variable flow through each of the arcs or give a chronological history of the particle flow through the system. Nevertheless, it is important to know that equations can give the same answers if they are developed correctly. The analytical method is usually a much easier and faster tool for securing the necessary information about a system; therefore, whenever it is possible to use it, by all means do so—the simulation can be too slow and too costly.

There are occasions, however, when no method other than simulation is available. When a total system has no analytical relationships—when there are no continuous variables—we cannot analyze the system with algebraic equations. A continuous variable is a variable that exists everywhere at some fixed interval and changes smoothly. Such a variable can be expressed in the form of an equation relative to some other variable. In reality, however, variables in most systems are not continuous; either they exist discretely, leaving gaps here and there, or they do not change smoothly. We are forced, in such instances, to admit that the only available technique is that of simulation—even though it may be nearly as difficult and as expensive as actually building the real process and analyzing it.

Who Should Simulate

Simulation can be a powerful tool when used by someone who is experienced with both the technique of simulation and the process to be simulated. A man familiar with a process can do a simulation of that process, even though he knows nothing about the technique of simulation. A man familiar only with simulation cannot possibly simulate correctly a process he does not understand. One of the major problems with computer simulation today is that there are many people who are familiar with the techniques of computer simulation but know little about the process that they are simulating. As a result, we have many simulations that give the wrong answers, and thereby give simulation a bad name.

6

The Computer and Simulation

THIS chapter covers the basic relationship between the computer and simulation—how the computer is used in simulation, how it relates to time and the real world, and how queues and flows are established and measured on a computer. We will learn how to make a computer program simulate an activity (a subprocess of a total process), and how the individual subprocesses can be connected together through a basic control mechanism and thereby made to simulate the entire process.

Real Time and the System

To begin with, we need to explore the concept of "real time." What is real time? It is exactly what it says it is—*real* time. The clock on the wall runs in real time. If someone were to change the gears in the clock it would run in nonreal time.

Let us assume that a computer program has been developed that will keep track of the quantity of any item in a company's inventory. There are hundreds of items that flow through the company each day, so that the on-hand amount for any item changes on a daily basis. We wish to monitor these on-hand amounts. The program has been written so that punch card information can be entered into the system to signal a change in a certain item. The punch card contains the item description, an identifier that tells the program whether the item is received into or withdrawn from the current stock on hand, and the actual quantity involved in the transaction. The program is designed to add or subtract the quantity involved in the transaction from the on-hand quantity. Thus we can interrogate the system to determine the current amount on hand of any item at any time.

The concept of real time comes into play at the point when the punch cards are entered into the system. If the cards are entered at the exact time of the real transaction, or shortly (within a few minutes) thereafter, the system is a real-time system, because the data recorded on the memory media are changing at almost the same time as the actual inventory is changing. If, on the other hand, the punch cards are all saved until sometime in the evening, and then entered into the system at the same time, the system is on nonreal time.

The example of the man riding a particle through a system used real time. An airlines reservation system, where the ticket agent has direct access to a computer through some type of keyboard or agent set, is a real-time system. We can define a simulated real-time system as a simulation of a real process, in which input to the simulated system is occurring in parallel with, or at the same time as, input to the real system.

The Simulation of Time

Time is one of the most important concepts in computer simulation. Not only must we know what things have happened during the simulation; we must also know when they happened, especially when they happened relative to other events. In addition to this, the basic simulation control mechanism must know what things are to happen and when they are to happen, so that the control can make them happen on schedule. Therefore, the *simulation of time* is a very important concept. How can we simulate time? We can take the time directly from a clock on the wall—which would, of course, be real time. We can count time in nonuniform increments from one event to another event when the interval of time between any two events is known but varies from event to event. We can also count time in uniform increments from some known event that occurs at fixed intervals. These are just a few of the methods available.

Let us now consider how a computer simulation works relative to time. We should be aware that a program running on a computer is a serial animal; it can do only one thing at a time and it does these things in a serial fashion. This would lead us to believe that a computer cannot simulate any process in which more than one thing is occurring simultaneously. If we had to simulate a process in real time, this would actually be the case, because we could not possibly schedule two events at the same time as we do in the real world. If we are to simulate a process correctly, however, we must allow for the fact that certain events do occur simultaneously. We can do this if we *simulate* real time by stopping time at points where two or more events must occur until those events have been scheduled. Once they are scheduled, time is started again. In this fashion we obtain the same effect as simultaneity.

Scheduling Parallel Activities

If we cannot schedule several events simultaneously, we cannot have them occurring simultaneously on the computer. The technique for handling this situation is to allow the events to occur serially on the computer when time is stopped. When all the events have occurred, we add to a "real-time clock" a fixed amount of time, which is equal to the duration of the longest activity in the group.

At this point, in both the real process and the simulation, the "vital system statistics" are, or should be, the same. Vital system statistics are such things as flow rates, queues, and total system throughput. During the interval of time when the activities are actually being performed on the computer, we cannot expect the vital system statistics to equal those of the real process. Therefore we must be certain that no other activities, especially system measuring activities, occur during that interval of time. When serializing certain parallel real activities in the process, we must be certain that we do not affect the system's vital statistics. If two or more of these parallel activities interact with each other in such a way that at their completion in a parallel operation the system's vital statistics are different from those in a serial operation, we cannot use this technique.

The Real-Time Clock

We will use a new tool, a "real-time clock," to implement our system. This clock will contain the real time in the system simulator, and it will be kept up to date by the control portion of the simulator. It has nothing to do with the clock on the wall, or with any clock in the computer hardware; therefore, it has no relation to the actual time. The clock is a simulated clock that contains the time at which certain important vital statistics in the real process will occur. In order to see how the clock works, let us assume that an activity is scheduled to start ten minutes from the current time and no other activity has to occur before it. We can add ten minutes to our real-time clock and start the activity, thereby passing over an interval of actual time in which nothing other than waiting would occur. When the activity is complete we can schedule the next activity, thereby saving real time that we may be able to use later, when we have to simulate time-consuming parallel activities from the real process in a serial fashion for our program.

We have not yet determined how to keep this clock up to date. What is the input to the clock? What is the thing or the mechanism that keeps the clock moving? The individual simulated activities themselves actually take care of this function. On the assumption that an isolated activity takes a given amount of time, we can periodically update the clock from the known time of the activities. The clock will move forward in uneven amounts of time on a calendar of scheduled events, with each activity scheduling another activity and entering it into the calendar. Associated with each event will be a time, always in the future, at which the event is scheduled to occur. The main control mechanism will search the calendar for the event that is scheduled to occur next and advance the clock to that time.

The Simulation of an Activity

The concept of time and the calendar of events leads us directly into the relationship between the computer and simulation. How does a computer simulate an activity? How does it simulate exactly the functions of some subprocess? The answer is that it does not. A computer *cannot* actually *duplicate* the continuous flow of liquid from a vat, because the computer is a discrete digital device. Its state in time is fixed, and remains fixed, until it executes a sequence of instructions that actually change the state. It cannot continuously simulate the volume of liquid in a tank that is being filled from three different sources, but it can compute these values in an incremental fashion from some known information about the flows.

If we know the flow rate with respect to time, for instance, we can compute the volume by multiplying the elapsed time by the flow rate for each source and totaling the individual contributions. By adding this total to the volume that was already in the tank, we can update the program. In this fashion, we can simulate the real flow and volume in the tank. Notice, however, that the simulation is correct *only* when the volume in the simulated tank changes, which is only at those times when the program is updated. We must be careful, therefore, to view or examine the volume in the tank only at the appropriate times; otherwise, we will get a false reading.

We should be aware that several things were actually simulated in this example. First of all, the volume in the tank was a fake. If we were to watch the volume in a real tank it would change continuously over time. In the computer, a memory location changed abruptly, sat still for awhile, and then changed again. Second, a real liquid was flowing into the tank in the real process. For the computer, we programmed a sequence of events in such a manner that after a certain interval of time the amount of flow was computed and added to the old volume, giving us a simulation of flow. Finally, time was also simulated. During the intervals of actual time when the simulated volume was not changing, the simulated time was not changing; time changed only when the simulated volume in the tank was brought up to date, at which point the clock was brought up to date.

The Simulation of a Process

We have seen how a digital computer can simulate a single activity. But how can it be used to simulate a total process? Each activity within a total process has an input and an output; the input to one activity is the output of one or more preceding activities, and the output from that activity, in turn, becomes the input to a succeeding activity. When we order the activities within the total process, what we do, essentially, is tie the inputs and the outputs together, and let the activities themselves create a flow.

In the computer we do essentially the same thing; we place the output from one activity into the input queues of its related succeeding activity. This seems simple enough, but how does an individual activity get control on the computer so that it can process some of its own queue and then pass the queue on to the next activity? This is usually accomplished by a special program, called the control program, and a calendar of events.

A program on a computer is a sequence of instructions that the computer hardware steps through one at a time until it reaches the end; it cannot execute the instructions simultaneously. It could not be any other way, because the program itself is written step by step; the result of any one step is used as an operand in the next step, and we cannot expect to get significant results if each step is executed independently of the previous step. The calendar of events is in the computer memory, and is a list of things to do and the time at which to do them according to the simulated clock.

The total system is set up in such a manner that, as a rule, an individual activity program will enter an event and the time at which it is to occur, into the calendar of events. Normally, the activity will also reschedule itself to occur again on the computer at some later time when it will examine its input queue and determine the total volume of input. Using a formula or other technique, the activity will compute the amount of the input queue that it could have processed in the elapsed time, and move that amount on to the next activity's queue. As we discuss this technique, keep in mind that we are covering only the general rule; there are many variations.

After processing some throughput, an activity usually schedules itself again in the calendar and then relinquishes the computer to the control program. The control program searches the calendar for the event which must be scheduled to occur at the earliest time from the current time, eliminates that event from the calendar, advances the real-time clock up to that time, and then relinquishes control to the event or activity.

In this fashion we see how simulated time moves along and how events continuously cause themselves to reoccur at certain intervals of time. Notice that we have done nothing to stop several events from scheduling themselves to reoccur at the same time. In such a situation, the control program will yield control to one event, wait for the control to return, and then yield control to another activity. Because both events were scheduled to occur at the same time in the calendar, the real-time clock is advanced to that time, thereby allowing two events to occur simultaneously in simulated time. For just a brief moment, then, the system is held idle while multiple events catch up.

A Sample Problem

At this point it will be helpful to consider an extremely simple example of a simulation: to simulate traffic flow at the cloverleaf intersection of two highways, shown in Exhibit 6.1. Our primary concern will be with the northbound lane. Imagine that there is a bridge at the intersection, carrying the northbound and southbound traffic over the eastbound and westbound traffic. We want to know how long to make the approach ramps that lead into the northbound lane, so that traffic will not back up on the east- and westbound lanes below the bridge. We shall treat the approach ramps as queues which receive input from the east- and westbound traffic. We want to design the system so that the queues will not overflow.

A careful examination of the intersection shows us that we can break down the problem into several activities which generate traffic flow, several queues, and corresponding activities which move traffic through the queues. First of all, there will be queues on the two approach ramps. Generating flow into those queues will be activities which will simulate the

EXHIBIT 6.1

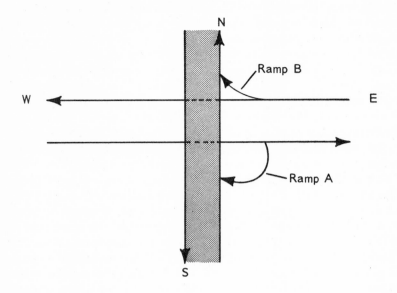

eastbound and westbound traffic, moving traffic out of the two queues will be two additional activities. There will be a third and a fourth queue, each of which will occur at a single position on the northbound highway at the exit position for both Ramp A and Ramp B. Only one car will fit in each exit position. Competing for this position will be a car in the northbound lane, immediately preceding the ramp, and the first car in each of the ramps. Cars in the northbound lane will receive priority over the ramp car; therefore, the ramp car will have to wait for the next unit of time to see whether it is clear to enter the position. There will be three additional activities which describe traffic flow in the northbound lane: one activity will simulate flow preceding Ramp B, one activity will simulate flow between Ramp B and Ramp A, and one activity will simulate flow beyond Ramp A.

Summing up the problem, we see that we have seven activities and four queues to simulate. The basic approach to handling this problem on a computer will be to develop seven independent programs to simulate the traffic flow into and out of the four queues. Each queue will be handled on the computer by the use of a single "word" location in memory. The technique will be to add one to the location when a car enters a queue, and subtract one when a car leaves a queue. We will allow the ramp queues to grow in size without restriction, as though the ramps were infinite in capacity. Later, when we find out how large the queue gets, we will design the ramp to hold that many cars. The third and fourth queues will have to be limited to values of zero or one, because these queues occupy a single position and can hold only one car at a time. Four single memory locations, then, will handle the four queues.

Now, let us consider how we can simulate two of the seven activities, the entrance of cars from the east- and westbound lanes into the ramp queues. There are many ways in which we can approach this problem. For instance, we can determine, by observation and statistical analysis, that one car enters the ramp every two minutes. Or we can develop a more sophisticated technique, in which we actually simulate the flow of traffic past the ramp, and determine which cars turn into the ramp and which cars continue forward, from a table of probabilities.

We can also extend this technique to include another table of probabilities to determine whether a car will be in a position to enter the ramp. Since there will not be an indefinite number of cars coming along the highway, we can expect some type of distribution of cars along that part of the highway that leads up to the ramp. We may find three cars packed tightly together and then seven vacant positions before another car enters that area. We can handle this with a table of 100 entries, where each entry will state either that a car is in the position or that there is no car in the position. The entries and their relative order can be determined by repeated, random observations of the first 100 car positions leading into the ramp.

Let us say that after 1,000 observations of the first 100 car positions, we find that there are 30 full positions and 70 vacant positions. We can then randomly place the 30 full and 70 vacant positions into the table of 100 entries. When we draw from the table, we are generating a random number from 1 to 100, and we can then check the corresponding memory location to see whether that position is full or vacant.

We have not yet defined what we mean by a car position. We will assume that cars are moving along at 50 mph, and that each car will normally travel no closer than five car lengths behind the preceding car. A position is the closest distance between cars under normal conditions, and we will assume that this distance is 100 feet. At 50 mph, cars will be moving at 72 feet per second, so that a new car will potentially be in position every $1\frac{3}{7}$ seconds. We draw from our table of 100 to determine whether a car is in the position; if one is, then we must determine whether it enters the ramp queue. This can be done by a forecast of the percentage of traffic that will enter the queue. If our forecast is for 25 percent, we can generate a random number from 1 to 100, and if the number we generate is not evenly divisible by four, we assume that the car did not enter the ramp queue.

We may well ask why we would choose to develop such an elaborate method of simulation, when, from our numbers, we could say that if traffic is 100 percent dense over an hour's period, a car enters the ramp queue on the average of one every $5\frac{5}{7}$ seconds during the peak traffic hour. We will see why we shouldn't use this technique if we apply it to the activity that takes cars out of the queue. If output from the queue is at a rate greater than $5\frac{5}{7}$ seconds, the queue will become infinite, in which case there is no sense in doing a simulation—we cannot possibly build an infinite ramp. If the output rate is less than, or equal to, $5\frac{5}{7}$ seconds, the queue will be zero—again there is no sense in doing a simulation. Given that the output flow is greater than, or equal to, the input flow, we know by experience that a zero queue is wrong. We all have also experienced queues building up on ramps, and yet, they do not become infinitely large; therefore, by using averages, we have arrived at the wrong answers.

Queues build for the very reason that averages are not what happen all the time; as a matter of fact, in some cases the average never occurs. For a period of time something greater than the average occurs, causing a buildup in the queue, and then, for another period of time something less than the average occurs, causing a reduction in the queues. Let this be a rule—in fact, let it be the first rule of simulation—never to use an average if it is possible to avoid it.

In line with this thought, a preliminary examination of the flow into and out of the ramp may save a considerable amount of time by eliminating the simulation altogether. If we find that the outflow cannot keep up with the inflow, we can forget the simulation, because we have already shown that the queue will be infinite. Only in the case where the average outflow is potentially faster than the average inflow will we find a simulation useful.

There are other ways in which to handle traffic flow into the ramp. We could, for instance, generate a random number from 1 to 100, and if the number is less than 70, assume that no car is in position to enter the ramp. If the number is greater than 70 we can assume that a car is in position to enter the ramp. This technique is a good one, if we have a good random number generator. This is not likely on a computer; generators are usually designed so that once a number appears, it cannot appear again until all the other numbers in the set have appeared. This is not truly random, but it often serves the purpose. In our case, however, it is not good enough; the numbers it would give us would present a problem similar to the averaging problem that we encountered previously. We will discuss random number generators in more detail in the next chapter; for now we will assume that we have a good one.

Now that we have developed a way to simulate traffic inflow into the ramp, we must decide how to implement it on the computer. The basic approach will be to write a special program which will determine, on the basis of the tables we have already discussed, whether a car is in position to enter the ramp. If a car is to enter the ramp, the program will increase the ramp queue by one, schedule itself to reoccur $1\frac{3}{7}$ seconds from the current time in the calendar of events, and then return to the control program. The control program will continuously scan the calendar of events searching for the next event that is scheduled to occur. It will then relinquish the computer to the program for that event, and wait for that program to return the computer. In this fashion, the activities will continue to get on and off the computer, creating the effect of continuous motion.

The second activity that we will simulate will be the traffic flow out of the ramp queue onto the crossover highway. Here we have a special case, depending on which ramp we are referring to. The outflow from Ramp B will be dependent upon the traffic flow leading up to the exit position of the ramp. This flow, in turn, has two components: the northbound flow leading up to Ramp A and the additional flow added to the stream by Ramp A itself. To begin, we will move a car out of the queue at Ramp B only if the car position that is adjacent to the ramp exit is vacant. We have determined that a car position equals 100 feet, and we will assume that there are 100 car positions between the two ramps. This can be simulated on the computer by using 100 memory locations, each of which will correspond to a car position. Locations marked "nonzero" will correspond to an occupied position. Locations marked "zero" indicate that there is no car in the position. We will move all positions up one every $1\frac{3}{7}$ seconds, and enter either a zero or nonzero value, depending on whether a car enters the queue. If a car enters from either the northbound lane or the ramp, we set the position to nonzero. If no car enters, we set the position to zero.

The activity which will move cars out of the ramp can be either an independent activity or a part of the activity that moves all 100 cars along the northbound lane between the two ramps. It can be part of that activity, because both activities potentially must move things every $1\frac{3}{7}$ seconds. There will be two criteria for moving a car out of the ramp queue: first, there must be a car in the ramp queue; second, the top position in the 100 position northbound traffic queue must be empty. If the position is empty, a car can be moved into it from the ramp queue, thereby decreasing the ramp queue size. The top position in the northbound queue is moved out of the queue and thrown away with each iteration, or each $1\frac{3}{7}$ seconds. Here again, the activity can be simulated by an independent computer program which works basically with two queues. One queue consists of 100 memory locations (the northbound traffic queue), and the other queue consists of one memory location which contains a numerical value equal to the magnitude of the ramp queue. The program can be written to manipulate these queues according to the circumstances of the line, and schedule itself in the calendar of events for reoccurrence every $1\frac{3}{7}$ seconds. Finally, it can return to the control program each time it completes the rescheduling of itself.

In addition to the independent simulation programs and the control program (which handles the calendar of events and the real-time clock), there will be what we call a background program. This program will be designed to give periodic "snapshots" of the various system queues, which will enable us to study the problem dynamics after completion of the simulation. The program will print out the size of the queues at various times during the run, and by studying the printouts, we should be able to determine what the maximum queues are. We may decide to design the ramps to handle only 80 percent of this queue, if it is at its maximum only for a few minutes during a peak two-hour period. This snapshot program will run under the control program in a manner similar to that of the activity programs, and, like the activity programs, will reschedule itself in the calendar of events. The control program will treat it exactly like an activity program, allowing it to gain control of the computer periodically, in order to print out information.

This, then, is roughly how we would handle a simulation of a traffic intersection. As we have pointed out, it is not the only way. We could have made all the queues similar to the northbound 100 position queue, and run a unique car through the intersection several thousand times, keeping track of its progress each time. Notice, however, that the ramp queues, as we designed them, will not permit unique identifications, because they give the numerical value of the queue rather than the exact position of each car in the queue.

7

Simulation Tools

In this chapter we will examine some of the basic tools of simulation, in order to develop a general idea of how we can implement a simulation on a computer. Specifically, we want to cover some of the standard requirements of simulators, simulation languages, and some of the basic hardware requirements needed to accomplish simulation.

The random number generator. In the preceding chapter, we referred, briefly, to random numbers and random number generators. As we become more familiar with simulation, we will find that random numbers are needed in almost all simulations. A random number generator is a device or a system that can produce a set of numbers in a given range, say, from 1 to 100. The device must be able to insure that every number in the range has an equal chance of occurring at all times. Such a system could be achieved by drawing a number from a hat and, after recording it, replacing that number in the hat. This would be as close to random as we could get. On the other hand, a system that produces a set of numbers in such a manner that once a number is drawn it cannot occur again until every other number occurs is not a good random number generator. Unfortunately, many random number generators on computers work in this fashion. A random number generator that produces the exact same set of numbers from one day to the next is not a good random number generator either.

What we need is a system that allows each number of a set an equal chance of occurring each time we use it (the same number can appear more than once before all the other numbers appear), and that does not produce a fixed repeating pattern of numbers. Actually, the first requirement is sufficient to achieve a random system, but, since we cannot achieve this on the computer, we must be satisfied with a system which will give us *numbers* that meet the two criteria.

In order to simulate the drawing technique on a computer, we could randomly put 100 numbers, from 1 to 100, into 100 sequential locations and draw these numbers from the stack one at a time. If we draw the first location first, the second location second, and so on, we will have drawn, after 100 draws, all the numbers from 1 to 100 without any repetition. What's more, we would then start again at the beginning and repeat the pattern. This would violate both of our criteria.

Let us try another approach by taking a number—say 4,823,542—dividing by 100, and taking the *remainder*, a two-digit number, as the random number. If we multiply this random number by a strange five-digit number—say 52,963—this gives us a seven-digit number that we can also divide by 100, which will leave us with a two-digit remainder and a new random number. This technique appears to be better, except that it will repeat itself each time we start the procedure on a new random number. In addition, once a given remainder appeared for the second time, the pattern would repeat itself. In this case some numbers might not be represented at all unless, by chance, the system produced all 100 numbers before one occurred twice, in which case, we would be in the same predicament we were with our first approach.

So we see that producing random numbers on a computer is an impossible task without some external human assistance. We should therefore develop a program that will be able to retrieve some program-independent data. Normally, a stack of punch cards containing random data is read into a machine which the program has access to. It is also possible to use the day clock or the real-time clock in the computer, on the assumption that the program is run at different times each day. This will give us truly random data, which, when coupled with a somewhat nonrandom computer technique, should give us what we want.

Suppose, for instance, that we took the value in the clock and, from it, produced a set of numbers ranging from 1 to 100. We could do this by writing a program that would produce a set of staggered numbers from 1 to 100 starting with the number in the real-time clock. Each time that we executed the program, we would get the effect of shifting the 100 numbers around, and, hopefully, changing their relative order. Then we could develop another program that would yield a single number from 1 to 100 every time it was executed, and would never yield the same number twice before it had yielded all 100 numbers. This number could be used to tell us how far down from the top of the "randomly" moving table (from the real-time clock) to go before we drew a number. This technique would provide as random a number as we are likely to get.

The probability distribution. Among the most frequently used tools in simulation are the probability distributions, and one of the most important of these is the normal distribution. What is a distribution? A distribution is a collection of events in which each event can be assigned a value. As an example, the sum value of throwing two dice can represent an event's value. If we plotted all possible values from throwing two dice, we would find that the values varied from 2 to 12, and that some values occurred more than once. The number 7, for example, occurs in 6 different ways, and there are a total of 36 different outcomes. We have, then, a set of 11 events, in which each event can be assigned a unique value. All the events constitute a distribution that has a range from 2 to 12, and a frequency that is based on the number of times each event appears in the distribution. We have plotted the distribution in Exhibit 7.1. Event 5 appears four times; therefore, we plot it with a frequency of 4.

We could also plot a distribution showing the range in the ages of people in a given area. In this case, we would find that the distribution would have a range from zero to 100, and we could ignore ages above 100 because of the small percentage of people in that category. The distribution would start off small, rise to a peak, and then fall off, possibly back to a zero level. We should have no trouble visualizing the plot of this age distribution; it would be similar in shape to the plot in Exhibit 7.1.

EXHIBIT 7.1

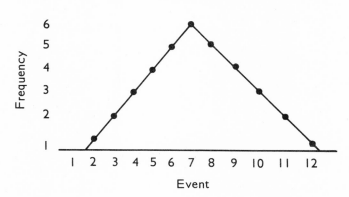

EXHIBIT 7.2

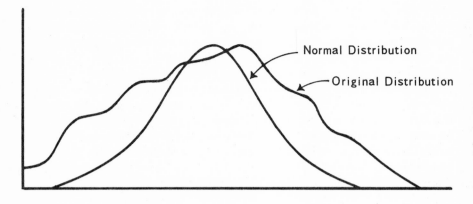

A normal distribution is similar to the distributions that we have discussed, except that it has a unique shape; a normal distribution is bell-shaped. It can be defined explicitly by a mathematical equation, which is of little importance to us. A normal distribution is arrived at by manipulating or transforming other distributions. If from any distribution we choose at random a set of values fewer in number than the original distribution, and we compute the average or the mean of the set, we can form a new distribution composed of all the averages from all the sets we have chosen. This new distribution will be normally distributed; it will have a range that is within the range of the original distribution, and it will have a mean value equal to that of the orginal. Exhibit 7.2 will help convey the idea. The bell-shaped normal distribution, contained within the uneven original distribution, was arrived at through statistical computation from the original distribution. Normal distributions are important, because it is much easier to determine mathematically the area under the resulting bell-shaped curve.

We could ask why, if the area under the curve is so important, are we interested in the normal curve rather than the original curve? The area under the curve represents the totality of events that can occur. Consider, for example, the diagram in Exhibit 7.3, which is rectangularly constructed to demonstrate more easily the principle involved. The area under the curve equals the sum of the heights of each event, as measured along the vertical axis. Event 2 is one unit high, event 3 is two units high, event 4 is three units high, event 5 is two units high, and event 6 is one unit high:

$$1 + 2 + 3 + 2 + 1 = 9 \text{ units.}$$

Since the area is equal to the totality of events that can occur, nine events can occur.

If we want to determine the probability that a random pick from the events will produce a certain event, we must divide the total possibilities into the total number of ways in which the event can occur. The probability that we would pick the event 3 is $\frac{2}{9}$, because there are two events with the value 3 in a total of nine events. If we are interested in the probability that a random pick will produce an event less than or equal to 4, we divide the total area into the area under the curve that has a value less than or equal to 4. This will give us a probability of $\frac{6}{9}$, which means there are six chances in nine that a random pick will produce a value less than or equal to 4. This tells us why the area under a curve is important; it is used to compute probabilities.

One reason for using the normal curve is that it can be defined nicely by an equation which allows us to construct a probability table. We can determine the probability of an event occurring by dividing the total area into the area up to the event in which we are interested.

In Exhibit 7.4, we can see that the probability of event c or less occurring is equal to the total area under the curve divided into the shaded area. In the table, we record the probability of c not as c but as an event that is b-c standard deviations from the center point b. We can apply these tables, which are computed for a normalized curve, by normalizing our own curve. Let us say, for instance, that our normal curve varies nine units to the left and right of the center point. We cannot use the tables directly, because they were computed for a curve that had deviated approximately three units to the left and right of the center point. We must therefore find what we call the standard deviation for our curve. By dividing the standard devia-

EXHIBIT 7.3

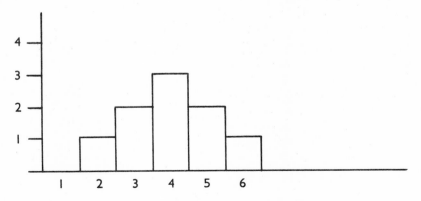

EXHIBIT 7.4

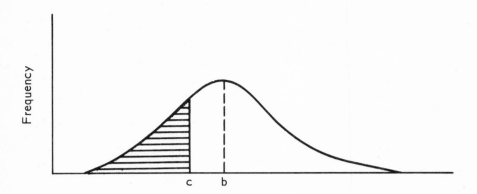

tion into the actual number of units an event is away from the center point, we can obtain the actual number of standard deviations that the event is away from the center point. We can then go directly to the normalized probability table to find the probability that a random pick will produce the event or some event less than the event.

A close examination of Exhibit 7.2 shows that the normal curve is a close approximation of the original curve. The closer the similarity the better, because we can then use the normal curve's probability tables to deduce things more accurately about the original curve, for which we have no tables.

We will find that our predictions become more reliable as our sample size becomes smaller. In fact, a sample size of one is perfectly reliable in that it will produce the original curve. But our problem is that because the original curve is not normal, it does not conform to the normal tables. On the other hand, a larger sample size will produce a more normal curve and will conform to the tables, but the resultant curve will not closely resemble the original curve. If we choose a sample size equal to the size of the original distribution, the resultant curve will be perfectly normal; in fact, it will have a single point which is equal to the mean of the original distribution. We must therefore choose a sample size small enough to give us a normal distribution with a variance or spread close to the original distribution. In summation, we use the normal curve because it lends itself to the standard tables and because, given the proper sample size, the resultant curve will be quite similar to the original curve.

To see how the normal probability distribution is used in simulation, let us look at a specific situation—the flow and speed of traffic at a given point on a highway. In our earlier example, we assumed that the average speed of a car approaching the exit ramp was 50 mph, and we converted this speed into time, which gave us $1\frac{3}{7}$ seconds between cars that were in position to enter the ramp. However, we made this computation on the basis that each car was moving at *exactly* 50 mph, rather than at an *average* speed of 50 mph. If we could somehow allow the speed of each automobile to vary, we could make the simulation more like the real process and thereby get more reliable results.

We can accomplish this by assuming that automobiles approach the ramp at a speed that varies between 35 and 65 mph, the average speed being 50 mph. We can assume the distribution of speeds to be normal or bell-shaped around 50 mph. Roughly speaking, the standard deviation for such a distribution would be equal to 5, because there are approximately 3 standard deviations from the mean to the extreme sides of a normal distribution. There is a 15-mph range from 35 mph to 50 mph; therefore we arrive at a standard deviation of $15\!/\!3 = 5$. If we use the probability tables in any statistical text or book of mathematical tables, we can arrive at the probabilities of the various speeds.

The entries in the tables represent the area under the curve from the center point; the concept is pictorially represented in Exhibit 7.5. To begin, we should determine the probability of a speed in a small range, say between 40 and 45 mph. We must subtract the area under the curve between 45 and 50 from the area under the curve between 40 and 50, and then divide this by the total area under the curve between 35 and 65. By using the probability tables we can avoid some extra work, because the tables are normalized; that is, the area under the curve is equal to one, and the entries in the tables are therefore the actual probabilities. By dividing our intervals by our standard deviation, we can normalize our own curve and therefore use the tables directly.

First, we compute the number of standard deviations between 50 and

EXHIBIT 7.5

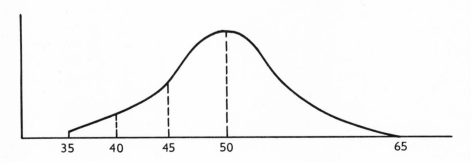

45 by dividing the interval by 5, our standard deviation. This gives us a standard deviation of 1. In a similar fashion we get 2 standard deviations between 40 and 50. From the tables, we get the corresponding entries for 1 and 2 deviations, and subtract the entry for 1 from the entry for 2, which will give us a positive value of less than 1. Let us assume the value is 2, which means that 20 percent of the cars will be moving at a speed between 40 and 45 miles per hour. Taking the midpoint of this speed, 42 mph, we can enter it randomly into a table with 100 positions.

In a similar fashion we can enter other speeds into the table according to their probability of occurrence. As we proceed with the simulation, a random draw from this new table will tell us when the next automobile will be in position to enter the ramp. This is an example of how a normal probability distribution can be used in simulation; it is an extremely useful tool. If we use the simulation technique extensively, we should find that we also make extensive use of normal probability distributions. If we do not, chances are that we are doing too much averaging.

It should be fairly obvious at this point that a considerable portion of the simulation is nothing more than moving things around from one stack or queue to another. The "things" may be such entities as cars, people, electrons, or cubic feet of liquid. We have a choice: We may either keep track of each entity uniquely, which would require a multiposition stack, or keep track of the quantity of entities. In the latter case we need only one position in the stack, an analogous situation to the ramp queue in the highway intersection simulation. In that example, we needed to keep track only of the quantity in the queue, not of the position in the queue, so that when a car entered the queue we only needed to add one to the value of the queue.

The multiposition stack. Often in simulation we are required to keep track of each entity's flow through the system; therefore, we must be able to isolate its position at any time. For example, traffic flow between the two exit positions of the two ramps is a multiposition stack or queue. In this type of stack, each entity is entered into the bottom position and is allowed to work up through the stack until it reaches the top and is removed. All entities within the stack move proportionately whenever the stack is moved up. The advantages of this type of stack are immediately obvious in a traffic flow situation, or in any case where the position of each entity, as either an absolute or a relative value, is important.

The FIFO stack. Another important type of stack or queue in simulation is a first in, first out (FIFO) stack. This stack is similar to the one that we just described, except that the space between any two objects in the stack is not important. We are concerned only that the relative order of all entries remain the same. The entities are entered into the bottom, and they work their way to the top and out as before. There were empty gaps in the multiposition stack, however; in this stack there are none. An analogy would be a line of people at a ticket window, where each person in the line goes to a different place or gate after he has received his ticket. We must therefore keep track of each person in the line, and where he will go when leaving the line.

The LIFO stack. There is one other type of stack that is important in simulation, a last in, first out (LIFO) stack. In this type of stack, things are entered into the stack from the top, thereby pushing everything else down, and then removed from the stack from the top, thereby moving everything up again—the last thing that goes into the stack is the first thing to come out. LIFO has practical implications in many warehousing applications.

These are basically the only types of stacks or queues that are used in simulation. Understanding how they work functionally and how they are implemented is a major step in understanding what simulation is all about. The best way to handle the stacking problem on the computer is to develop a general subroutine or subprogram that can either enter an entity into a stack or retrieve an entity from a stack. We can also enter certain arguments or parameters into the program. The parameters will tell the subprogram the name of the stack (the program will be working with many stacks) and the type of stack: LIFO, FIFO, and so forth. Developing this program to cover all stacks will be an important step in our simulation.

The simulated real-time clock. Another handy tool in simulation is the simulated real-time clock. This amounts to a single memory location in which we keep the current value of simulated time. Several different programs may update it, and almost all programs in the simulation will have access to it. Any program that is simulating some event in the system will require the clock, so that it can schedule itself to reoccur at some future point in simulated time. In addition, the clock can add a fixed increment of time to all the events scheduled to occur in the calendar, if a certain event must occur before but in serial fashion with the other events.

The snapshot program. Another important simulation tool is the snapshot program. This program periodically takes a "snapshot" of the system, and is used to analyze the system's behavior. Without the snapshot routine, we cannot determine how the system is behaving under dynamic conditions. The program is not actually part of the simulation; it is merely a piggyback or a background program that schedules itself to occur periodically in the calendar of events. This program usually causes a high-speed printer to print out all the system's queues. The program should be written so that it accepts as arguments or parameters the names of all the queues that should be printed out, and the frequency with which they should be printed. The program then rides piggyback in the simulation, like the event programs, and when it gets control from the control program, it prints out the appropriate queues or stacks and schedules itself to reoccur later.

8

Simulation Language

In order to understand any computer language, we must first understand how a computer works on a program. The computer hardware (electrical portion) is designed to sequence through a set of instructions serially, in the order written by the programmer. The instructions are things like add, subtract, multiply, shift, and move, and are called operators. A legitimate question here is add what, or subtract what, or move what and where? From the nature of these instructions, we can clearly deduce that there must be some values involved, or things to be operated on—these we call operands. The operators and the operands are both loaded into the memory device and are called the computer software. The term "software" dates back to the early 1950s and encompasses, roughly, the "changeable" portion of the entire system. In other words, it is supposed to be easier to change the software than to change the hardware—the hardware being the printed circuit cards, the back panel wiring, the memory, and the power supply.

We said earlier that the program instructions are read in sequential order into the memory from the punch cards. We certainly can understand that the first card would be read through the reader first, the second card second, and so forth. But we may wonder what happens to this information in the computer memory. The memory is also sequential; it has a finite number of cells or locations, each of which has a unique address. As we read the cards into the memory, they are stored in these sequential memory locations. In other words, the information punched on the first card is stored in memory at an address that is lower (numerically) than the address of the second card. The second card immediately follows the first card and has an address lower than the third card, and so forth.

Once the program is loaded, we place the memory address of the first instruction in a register and then start the computer. The computer hardware executes the instructions, in the order in which they occur in memory, at high speed (about one million per second), until it encounters a "stop" instruction. Sometimes a programmer can work for years, developing several thousand instructions, only to see the computer sail through them in less than a second. We must understand that all this is an oversimplification of what actually happens. In the early 1950s, some computers were almost this simple. Today, although many refinements have been made that make the computer much more complicated, the basic principles are still the same.

Loops in the Program

We can add one instruction that makes the program much more practical. This is the branch instruction; it tells the computer to break the sequence and go somewhere other than the next sequential memory location to find the next instruction. The instruction can also work on a conditional basis. For example, an instruction might be as follows: "If the content of a memory location is zero, branch to another location. If it is not zero, go to the instruction in the next location." This instruction will carry with it the address in memory where the next instruction will be found if the first condition is met. The inclusion of this instruction makes the computer practical, because so-called repetitive loops can be programmed and executed thousands of times. This enables us to command the program to repeat certain trivial numerical tasks any number of times without having to rewrite the program steps over and over again.

Binary—the Computer's Language

We are now in a position to discuss some of the programming languages. It is usually best to interact with the computer at as high a level as possible. The computer itself works purely in binary, even if the marketing brochure says it is a decimal machine. Writing programs in binary forces us to work on the computer problem, instead of on the problem for which we initially decided to write the program.

The basic problem is that we want to communicate in an English-oriented language, but the computer understands only binary. The problem is solved by writing, in binary, an "interpreter" program which will accept a limited number of English-oriented statements, and generate a binary set of instructions from them. We call this program a compiler. Thus between our program and the computer is the compiler, which interprets our English statements into binary instructions which the computer can act upon. We are now prepared to discuss some of the higher-level languages that are available to help us simulate.

FORTRAN as a Simulation Language

First of all, let us cover FORTRAN language, which was not initially developed for simulation, but is a language which can be used for simulation quite easily. In fact, most other languages that have been developed specifically for simulation were written in and based on FORTRAN. One of the best things about FORTRAN is that it is probably the easiest computer language to learn, because it consists of four essential English-oriented instructions. The four instructions, or "verbs" as they are called in the trade, are DO, IF, =, and GO TO. With these four statements, we can program anything that can be programmed in any computer language including binary.

The = statement. In FORTRAN, this statement, along with certain other information, is punched on a single punch card. As an example, the expression $A = B$ tells the compiler to produce a set of binary instructions that will cause the value of memory location B to be placed in memory location A. Let us assume that the compiler has assigned the address 1000 to A, and the address 2000 to B. When the compiler encounters the statement $A = B$, it generates a set of computer binary instructions that move the contents of memory location 2000 into memory location 1000.

The = statement will also function with other operators, such as $+$, $-$, $\div$, and $\times$, so that we can perform basic arithmetic operations. A statement like $A = B + C$ then becomes legitimate. The compiler will add B to C and put the total in A. As a matter of fact, we can string out the expression on the right side to a multiple number of terms and operators. We call A, B, and C variables. What they really amount to are memory locations.

We can also refer, in FORTRAN, to multivalued lists. A by itself is a single memory location. If we subscript A such as $A(I)$, it means that A is a table, or a list of sequential things, in memory. $A(1)$ is the first location in the table. $A(2)$ is the second location, $A(3)$ is the third, and so on. Using the subscripted concept we can write things like $A(I) = B(I)$ where the compiler assigns to I a numerical value equal to whatever location I is set to. If I is equal to 3 then the statement becomes $A(3) = B(3)$ or the third entry down into the B table in memory is to be moved into the third entry down in the A table.

The IF statement. This instruction allows for conditional branching in the program, and could appear on a punch card as IF(A) 100, 200, 300. It tells the compiler to examine the contents of memory location A, and, if the location is negative, to generate an instruction that will cause the computer to branch to statement 100; if the A is zero, to go to 200; and if A is positive, to go to 300. What are 100, 200, and 300? These are numbers which the programmer can assign to his FORTRAN statements by punching the numbers in preassigned columns of the statement cards (columns 1–5). In this fashion the programmer can uniquely define each of his statements. The numbers in the example are arbitrary; the programmer can use any numbers he chooses.

Inside the parentheses, right after the IF, we chose A as the value to be checked by the compiler. This can actually be any value, such as B, or $A(I)$, or $A(5)$. The expression inside the parentheses can even be arithmetic such as $[A(I)-B(I)]$.

The DO statement. This instruction tells the compiler that all the statements following the DO statement down to a specific statement are to be repeated a certain number of times. The statement at which the repeated loop is to stop and the number of times the loop is to be repeated are both specified in the DO statement. The format for such a statement is:

$$DO\ 500\ I = 1,\ 100$$

This statement tells the compiler that starting with the next statement, and down to a statement which is labeled 500, the compiler should generate a code such that the computer will continue to repeat the statements in that segment until the value I is equal to 100. The initial value of I is 1. As an example, consider these three FORTRAN statements:

$$200\ DO\ 500\ I = 1,\ 100$$
$$300\ A(I) = 0$$
$$500\ B(I) = 0$$

Statement 200 tells the compiler to repeat statement 300 and 500 while the subscript I varies to 100 starting from 1. The effect of this segment of statements is to clear to zero all the values in the two tables A and B. The compiler will generate a code that tells the computer to set $I = 1$ initially, then to go to statement 300 and set $A(1) = 0$, and then to go to statement 500 and set $B(1) = 0$. After that the computer will test I to see whether it is at 100. Because it is not, it will step I up by 1, go back to statement 300, and set A(2) = 0 and B(2) = 0. Notice that the subscript I has a value of 2 during the second time through the code. The computer again tests for I = 100, finds that it is not, steps I up by 1, making it 3, and goes back to statement 300. This is continued until I = 100, at which time the computer moves on to the statement following 500.

The GO TO statement. This simple instruction has the format:

GO TO 700.

This statement causes the computer to go to the statement with the label 700, instead of going to the statement immediately following the GO TO statement. With the exception of some statements designed to get input into and output out of the computer, and some others designed essentially to give information to the compiler rather than cause the computer to do something, this is our basic vocabulary.

Who would have thought that four types of statements in a programming language would be sufficient to cause the computer to do everything it can do in its own language? Most computers, by the way, have about 100 types of instructions they can handle. The user has a choice; he can study the 100 computer instructions, learn all about each one, and then write programs in considerable detail; or he can learn the four FORTRAN statements discussed here and then write the program. To give an idea of the magnitude of the difference between these two approaches, if we wrote in machine code the three-statement program shown earlier it would require about 15 instructions. Each of the instructions would be much more difficult to learn than FORTRAN, and it would take about five to ten times as long to debug the machine-coded program than it would to debug a FORTRAN program.

The Preparation of a Program

Let us proceed to some simulation techniques using FORTRAN. To begin, we will handle a simple type of stack that will require a subprogram. When called, the subprogram will retrieve the top entry in the stack, put it in a location called TOP, and then move all entries in the stack up by one. The program steps are as follows:

```
10   TOP = STACK(1)
20   DO 30 I = 1, LAST
30   STACK(I) = STACK(I + 1)
40   LAST = LAST − 1
50   GO TO RETURN
```

These five steps accomplish all the requirements for retrieving the next entry out of a stack. The statement labeled 10 causes the computer to pick up the first entry in the stack, symbolically called STACK, and moves it into a location called TOP. The statement at 20 tells the compiler to repeat all the steps beyond this step down to step 30, and vary the value I from 1 up to the value given in the symbolic memory location LAST. If the contents of memory location LAST was equal to 25, I would vary from 1 to 25. As will be seen later, LAST contains the actual count of the number of entries in the stack.

Each time the instruction at 30 is repeated the value I is incremented by one so that I goes from 1 to 2 to 3 and so forth up to 25. The statement at 30 causes the $(I + 1)$ entry in the stack to be moved up one to the Ith entry in the stack. Because the step is covered in the DO statement's range, it is repeated on every entry in the stack. The total effect, therefore, is to move all entries in STACK up by one.

Let us examine the statement carefully. The first time the step is executed, $I = 1$, and therefore the statement essentially says $STACK(1) = STACK(2)$. The 2 in the parentheses on the right comes from $I + 1 = 1 + 1 = 2$, since I initially is 1. This causes the compiler to move the entry in STACK at 2 up to 1. The next time through, the compiler increments I by 1, which now makes the statement at 30 say $STACK(2) = STACK(3)$. This causes the third entry in the stack to be moved up into the second position in the stack. The same procedure is continued until the 25th time, when $STACK(25) = STACK(26)$, which is the last move. From here the computer leaves the step at statement 30 and moves down the sequence to the statement labeled 40.

The statement at 40 decreases the count of the number currently in the stack. Because we took one out, we decrease by one the symbolic location in memory which contains the actual count of the current number in the stack. If there were 25 in the stack before, now there are only 24. Notice that the statement is inconsistent algebraically, but keep in mind that LAST is the name of a memory location, not the actual variable itself. The variable is the value of the contents of the location whose symbolic label is LAST.

The Memory Locations

It is appropriate at this point to review the memory addressing concept. Recall that each location in memory has associated with it a unique numerical address. When the compiler codes the program written in FOR-TRAN language, it encounters all these symbolic names that correspond to memory locations. There are no numerical addresses in FORTRAN, but numerical values must be assigned to the symbolic names for the computer. This is done by the compiler in an arbitrary fashion. The programmer does not care which numerical values are assigned to the symbolic names as long as the values are unique and consistent. This means that after the compiler has assigned a memory location to a name, whenever it encounters that name again it must use the same address. As an example, let us assume that LAST is assigned memory location 1000, and that somewhere else in the program we have occasion to increase LAST whenever we make an entry into STACK. At this point, it is important for the compiler to remember that it has already assigned 1000 to LAST, and that it must therefore use that value again. All the symbolic names are handled in a similar fashion in FORTRAN.

The statement on line 50 tells the compiler to cause the computer to branch to a statement at a line specified in the contents of the symbolic memory location RETURN. The contents of memory location RETURN is set to a desired return point just before line 10. Let us assume that we wish to return to the step at line 300, right after retrieving the top entry out of the stack. In this case we would set RETURN to 300 and then go to line 10.

We have done a lot of talking about the contents of a memory location, but we haven't really defined what it is. The contents of any memory location in a computer is merely a numerical value that can never be below zero, and never be above some large value—say 10 million. How then can we store such things as the names of people, the names of events, or the names and types of cars? The answer is that we can store them only to the extent that we can assign each of these things a unique number. We know this can be done on a large scale, as evidenced by the fact that the Bell System changed the alphabetic prefix codes to numerical codes—to the regret of many.

The Calendar of Events

Let us now explore how we can handle the calendar of events with FORTRAN. To begin with, we must understand that a calendar must include space for both the name of the event and the time when the event is to occur. Let us assume that the calendar is composed of a two-dimensional rectangular array with a width of two words or columns and a depth of 100. This will provide room for up to 100 events in the stack simultaneously. The first of the two columns will contain the name of the event; the second will contain the time the event is to occur. We'll give the stack the symbolic name EVENT and address it with this name. The program steps required to search out the next event to occur in time are as follows:

```
10    NEXT = 2400
20    DO 60 J = 1, LAST
30    IF [EVENT(2, J) − NEXT] 40, 60, 60
40    K = J
50    NEXT = EVENT(2, J)
60    CONTINUE
70    NAME = EVENT(1, K)
80    TIME = EVENT(2, K)
90    DO 110 I = K, LAST
100   EVENT(2, I) = EVENT(2, I + 1)
110   EVENT(1, I) = EVENT(1, I + 1)
120   LAST = LAST − 1
130   GO TO BACK
```

This general sequence of instructions provides for finding the event that is to occur next in time, putting the name of the event in a location called NAME, and then entering the time at which it is to occur in a location called TIME. The basic idea is to search every entry in column 2 of the calendar and find the entry with the smallest value. This value corresponds to the time of the next event. After the name and time have been put into NAME and TIME, the program will go back and push up all the entries in the stack below the entry that was just removed. Finally, the program will decrease by one the number of entries in the stack, so that the next time through the program we will know how many entries remain in the stack.

At line 10 we assign the value of 2400 hours to NEXT, which means that NEXT is the last thing to occur; therefore, everything in the stack should occur before 2400. At line 20 we set up a DO loop, from line 30 to line 60, which will find the smallest time in the stack. At line 30 we check to see whether the difference between the first entry in the stack and 2400 is negative. If it is, we know that it will occur before 2400 and is therefore the smallest entry so far. Now we go to line 40, where we set K = J (which is 1) and then change NEXT to equal the time at which this event is to occur. At line 60 we continue the DO loop by going back to line 30, incrementing the value of J to 2 and reexecuting statement 30. This time, however, the second entry in the time stack is compared with the earliest time so far (NEXT). If the time of the second entry is found to be smaller, we go to 40; if it is not smaller we go to 60 and continue with the next comparison.

The two statements at 40 and 50 are executed whenever we find an event that is due to occur before the earliest scheduled event encountered so far. Executing the two statements causes the new time to be placed in NEXT. In this loop, then, NEXT contains the time of the earliest scheduled event in the stack. After we have gone through the loop the number of times specified in LAST, we go to statement 70. At 70 we pick up the name of the event which has the earliest time in the stack, that is, the Kth event, place it in NAME, and place the time of its occurrence in TIME at line 80. At line 90 we set up a DO loop down to 110 where, starting from the Kth entry we move all the entries in the stack, down through the LAST entry, up one position. This fills the blank spot left by the entry which was removed. At 120 we decrease the count of entries in the stack by one, and at 130 we return to whatever value was assigned to the location BACK.

This sample program for handling the calendar of events in a simulator model should give us a better feel for how we can apply simulation to the computer. We have seen that FORTRAN programming is relatively simple and that it interfaces with the computer at a fairly high level. As mentioned before, some higher-level languages were designed specifically for simulation, and most of these languages either are programmed in FORTRAN or allow the user to code in FORTRAN. These higher-level simulator languages do much of the stack handling, random number generation, and generation of the probability distributions for the user. This allows us to concentrate on the actual simulation. Once the detailed repetitive type of programming is complete, simulation is relatively easy; it simply becomes a problem of moving things around from one queue to another.

9

Simulation Applied to the Computer

This chapter covers several sample applications for simulation that illustrate its practical implementation. Probably in no other science is implementation more important than in simulation. There are infinitely many ways to simulate any single event. It is in the implementation where we separate the men from the boys. Two basic things provide a measure of a person's ability to simulate a problem. These are a clear and concise understanding of the real system to be simulated and a logical mind. The simulation of a problem requires a person who can see to the bottom of a problem and likes to figure out what makes things work. Strangely enough, this type of person does not usually have the slightest interest in the actual answers; he is more interested in the correct and precise formulation of the problem. This must be taken into consideration, because to complete an effective simulation we should have a person who also takes a practical interest in the results and will carry out the final implementation of the system.

To be of use, every simulation must have an objective. Without the objective the simulation becomes useless; its value for the simulator is merely esthetic. We must learn, then, to make the objective of the simulation an integral part of the problem. The objective might be, for example, to minimize some value or to maximize the value of some variable. Keeping this in mind at the outset will help immensely in completing the job effectively. Let us now proceed to several examples of where and how simulation can be put to use, keeping in mind as we go that the idea is to show not only where and how it can be used but, most important of all, for what reasons.

Let us start with the simulation of a hamburger shop for a national chain operation. The objective will be to determine certain variables so that operating cost and initial capital investment in plant and equipment can be minimized. Without prior knowledge of simulation, we might say, "What do you mean minimize cost? We'll just eyeball the whole thing and make it as competitive as possible." Some might even say, "There is no minimum. Any way we set it up, it will come out the same." This, of course, is not true. There *is* a difference, and there *is* money to be saved. It would, for instance, be a foolish waste of money to provide benches and tables enough to seat a thousand people simultaneously, and then to provide only one window at which all these people must pick up their food. The idea, then, is to find the right balance of plant, equipment, and personnel so that we do not waste resources.

We can start this particular analysis by developing a plan or design for the flow of people through the shop. After the design is completed, we can simulate it to determine the size of various queues in the shop, given a normal inflow of customers. The results will enable us to determine how we can maintain a balance among the queues and thereby save on both operating cost and initial equipment cost. This meets our minimum criteria for a simulation: we now have something to simulate and a reason for simulating it.

The diagram in Exhibit 9.1 represents the basic design concept and shows how people will move through the shop. In this particular example there are four main points of interest. To simulate the front door, labeled 1 in the diagram, we have to develop some type of distribution which will tell us whether somebody is coming through at a particular time. After people come in through the door they will move into a waiting queue which will snake around metal railings in the direction shown by the arrows until they reach the order window, labeled 2 in the diagram. In this area a queue will be created because of the delay introduced into the system at 2.

After leaving the order window, each customer will move to point 3, where he will pick up his order. The pickup window will often introduce additional delays into the system, thus making the waiting lines longer. We must therefore determine how long each customer must wait at both station 2 and station 3. If a customer places a large order, it will take

EXHIBIT 9.1

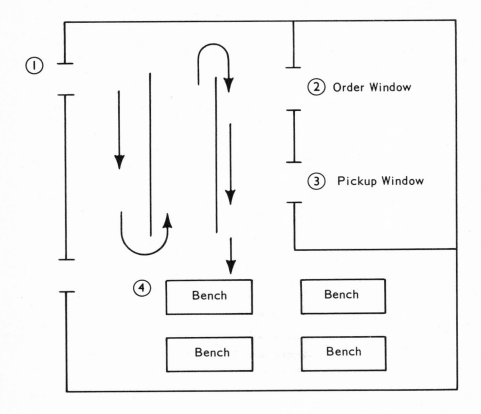

①
② Order Window
③ Pickup Window
④ Bench
Bench
Bench
Bench

longer to serve him at both stations. If the customer places a strange order for food that is not already prepared the waiting time will be further increased, thereby increasing the queue.

At these two stations, then, we want to be sure to have both sufficient help and the proper equipment so as to keep the queues at a minimum and customer flow at a maximum. Otherwise, if we continuously allow long queues, customers will stop coming and thereby lower our business. In addition to these problems, we have the problem of seating the people. We wish to know how many benches and tables will be needed to seat all the customers and what the maximum queue at point 4 will be.

We can begin to tackle the problem by developing an overall flow chart for the simulation, as well as flow charts for the problem areas. These four flow charts give only a general idea of how the overall program will work. They are incomplete, the most noticeable omission being a program for the queue at station 3. The detailed programming techniques were covered in the preceding chapter—what is important here is the overall picture of how the simulation will be developed and what the flow will be.

The main program is shown on the flow chart in Exhibit 9.2, beginning with a circle labeled START. First, we initiate all subprograms; then we search through the calendar of events to find the event which is to occur earliest. In the next box, we SET CLOCK equal to that time, and then we GO TO that event. After the event has been executed, we return to the RETURN point, at which time the main program goes to the circle la-

EXHIBIT 9.2

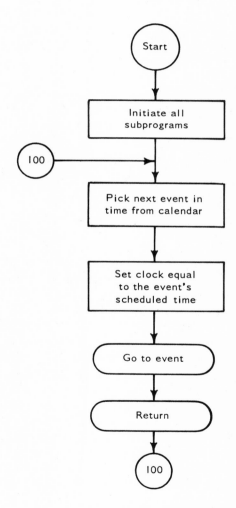

beled 100. Notice that 100 is also indicated farther up on the chart. We return and repeat the process, first searching the calendar for the next earliest event to occur. This process continues throughout the simulation.

The next flow chart, Exhibit 9.3, is the main entrance program simulation. First we pick a random number from a prestored table, to determine whether a customer is coming through the door in this time interval. If someone enters, we increase the line queue by one. The table is based on observations made at 30-second intervals at similar hamburger shops.

EXHIBIT 9.3

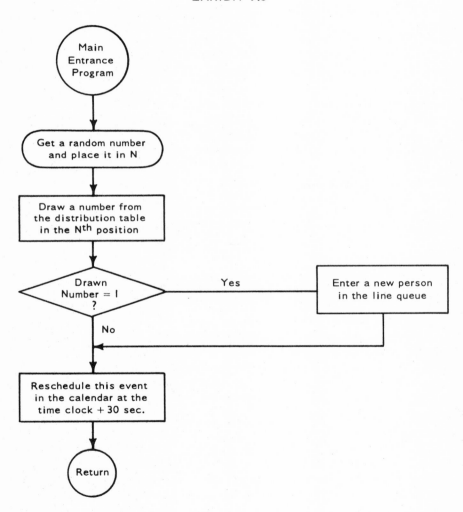

Let us assume there is one chance in five that a customer will enter the door during a 30-second interval at a busy hour. We might build a table of 100 entries, with 20 of the entries set at 1 and the other 80 set at zero. If we draw a 1, a customer enters; if we draw a zero, no customer enters. On occasion we can randomly move the entries around in this table. For a complete simulation project we should consider compiling another table that could be used during nonrush hours. For the purposes of this sample, however, we are concerned with being prepared for the worst case—the rush hour.

The main entrance subprogram starts with the drawing of a random number, ranging from 1 to 100, which is then placed in N. Next we draw from our 100-entry distribution table of ones and zeros the Nth entry. At the next step we make a decision: If the draw is a 1, we go along the YES path; if the draw is zero, we go along the NO path. If we follow the flow chart in Exhibit 9.3 we can see that if we are on the YES path, we increment the LINE waiting queue by one and end up back on the NO path which takes us to the final step. This tells us to reschedule the event 30 seconds later in the calendar of events and then sends us on to the RETURN point of the main program, which we have already described.

Next we go to the order window program in Exhibit 9.4. Here we use a new technique to determine how long a person will be delayed at the window. As we have discussed previously, an extra element of delay in the system can occur here because of excessively long orders or special orders that require additional time to submit, fill, and pay for. We enter the program from the main program at the circle that says order window program. We move down to a point where we draw a random number from 1 to 3, and then proceed through a series of branch points at which we make a decision. At the first branch point, we check the number to see whether it is 1. If it is, we move along the YES path; if it is not, we proceed down the NO path, where we check the number to see whether it is 2, and so forth. Whenever we find a match, we proceed along the path indicated, to which we have set a DELAY value of 30, 50, or 60 seconds. After the DELAY has been set, we proceed to the step where we decrease the line queue by one and increase the pickup queue by one. Next, we reschedule this event in the calendar to occur CLOCK + DELAY seconds later; the current time is CLOCK, and to arrive at a time later than CLOCK we must add the DELAY time to it.

The last flow chart, Exhibit 9.5, shows the final queue in the system, where people are waiting to find a place to sit down and eat. We want to keep this queue at a minimum, but we do not want to have an excessive investment in benches and tables. The overall approach is to assign to each person entering the table area a random amount of time from 5 to 15

EXHIBIT 9.4

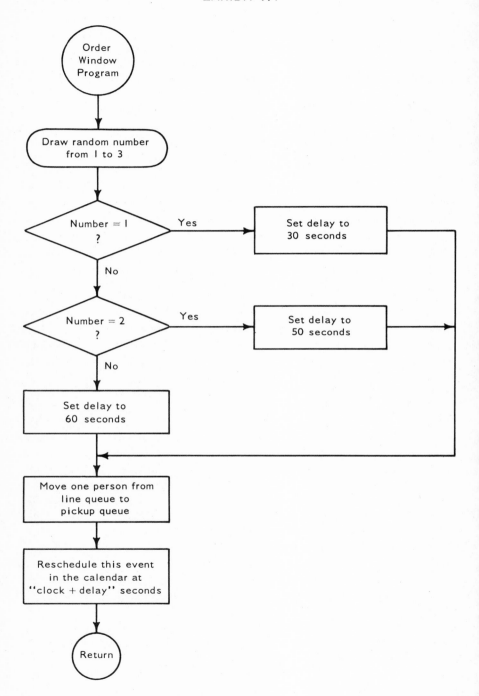

EXHIBIT 9.5

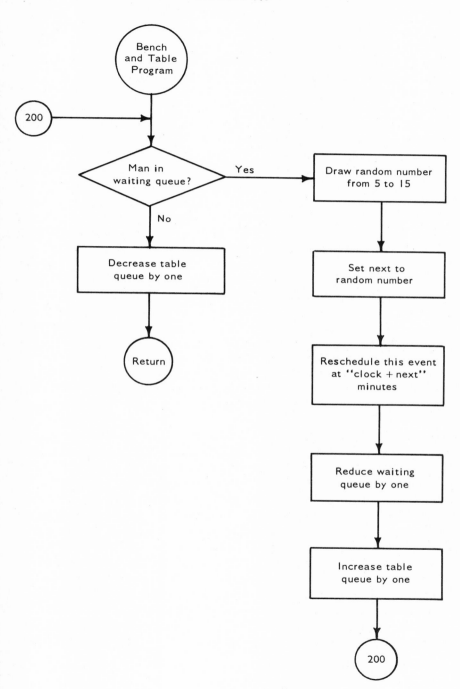

minutes, which corresponds to the length of time it will take him to eat. This subprogram is activated, we recall, by the main program. The fact that it is now running indicates that an event scheduled earlier—to move a customer out of the shop—is now due to occur.

The program then searches the calendar of events and finds that the next event scheduled to occur is to check the bench and table program. This subprogram immediately checks to see whether anyone is waiting to get a table. If so, we move along the YES path to the right, where we draw a random number from 5 to 15, then set the memory location NEXT equal to the random number. Next, we schedule this program to reoccur at a time in the future equal to CLOCK + NEXT minutes. We decrease the table waiting queue by one, increase the bench and table queue by one, and then go up to point 200, where we check again to see whether there are any more customers waiting to get into the tables. If there are no more customers waiting, we follow the NO path down to the box where we decrease the table queue by one, which simulates a person leaving, and then return to the main program.

This fairly well covers all the flow charts. Notice, however, that we are missing not only the pickup window queue, and possibly certain other queuing areas that were not introduced, but also a snapshot program to print out the contents of all the queues periodically. Such printouts can be used to study the queuing effect in the shop, and can possibly be helpful in determining the required number of employees, amount of equipment, and size and number of tables in the bench and table area. We might also consider having the snapshot program condense the information into an hourly average before printing (rather than printing out every five or ten minutes), thereby cutting down on the printer output and speeding up the run on the computer.

Using this technique, we could simulate thousands of actual operational hours in a matter of minutes—probably as fast as a printer could print out the information. Most printers print at rates in excess of 300 lines per minute, which would mean that in three minutes we could print out 900 lines, each line containing the simulated hourly average of each of the shop queues. This would correspond to 900 hours of operational experience, with no investment in plant and equipment.

The entire job would probably require no more than 200 FORTRAN statements which a good programmer could design, write, debug, and document for a computer in about one month. The cost for running the computer for about three minutes would be approximately $5, which is not bad for 900 hours' worth of operational experience.

There are many other areas where simulation can be of help in designing systems. Let us explore some of these areas very briefly in the remainder of this chapter. First let us consider a supermarket, which has a potentially great number of queues and bottleneck areas. To begin with, we have a parking lot problem; we want to make the parking lot large enough to turn customers away very infrequently, if we decide to turn them away at all.

In the store we have people moving down the aisles with their carts, and they will stop occasionally to pick up some product, possibly creating a queue along the aisle. We may expect that on occasion two people will stop adjacent to each other, thereby blocking the aisle completely for a few seconds. This also will have an impact on the flow of people through the store. In simulating the aisle flow, we should assign the various products a specific position along the aisle. We should then assign to each product a probability of being picked.

As an example, if we place all the catsup in one area, it should be safe to assign a probability of .6 that a person adjacent to it would stop his cart and pick up a bottle. If we placed the mustard just across the aisle, we could expect that this particular area in the store might be subject to some queuing. We could avoid this by placing a relatively lower probability item across from a high one.

We would move the people along the aisles at uniform speeds, with each maintaining his position relative to the others unless he or someone in front of him stopped for a product. This part of the program would be retriggered automatically—say, every five seconds. When we moved a person, we would move him about three feet forward, unless he was queued. With this technique we can learn where the potentially dangerous queuing areas are and possibly rearrange the products so as to minimize aisle queuing, thereby speeding the customers through. The logic here is that if the store is too crowded or it takes a customer too long to shop, he will not return. This is especially true when the competition down the street has the same products at about the same price.

After moving through the aisles, the customer moves onto the checkout lanes. Here, of course, we all know that he must wait, and this is probably the most dangerous queue in the store, as far as losing the customer is concerned. With every minute that he stands in this line, we increase the probability of losing the customer. Ideally, the object would be to have a sufficient number of counters and operators to keep the queues at zero and yet keep every operator 100 percent busy. Unfortunately, customers seem to come in bunches, not in a smooth, even flow, and the checkout time for each customer varies. The waiting time is therefore longer in certain queues than in others of the same length. The object should be to try to determine the maximum number of checkout counters required to handle the heaviest traffic and the number of operators required for each four-hour interval. In this fashion, the number of operators will vary from one four-hour period to another as the day progresses.

Finally, we must consider the problem of how to get the groceries to the cars in the parking lot. Here again, speed must be an important criterion. We have all experienced many different methods used by different stores for getting the groceries to the cars. Each technique has a different cost and a different queuing problem. Simulating the whole supermarket system before actually designing and constructing the building and the parking lot could well pay off for the investor. The total cost of the simulation would probably be less than $5,000.

One of the most ironic applications for simulation is simulating the computer system itself, to evaluate computer timing requirements. Given a certain set of jobs that are to run on a computer, we might want to know what kind of computer we should buy or rent. Or it might be most practical for us to rent the time we need on a service-center computer. There are in existence today many so-called computer simulation programs that analyze a customer's problems and help him decide which computer he should get. For the most part, however, these are not actually simulations. Exactly what they are is beyond the scope of this book, but they have been extremely lucrative for the companies that sell the service. It should be clear that if you are going to buy a computer or any other complex system, and you wish to do some simulation, you should have the help of a man who is thoroughly familiar with the system and the job requirements.

Let us assume we have three types of jobs to run on a computer. We want to decide how much computer time the jobs would require on each of several computers. Our object is to decide which computer does the best job. Let us assume that the jobs are payroll, inventory control, and accounts payable and receivable. Each of these jobs, when finally programmed, will have some internal characteristics which will determine its total running time. We could start the analysis by flow-charting the job generally, then separating out in the flow charts the times when we are actually running on the computer and the times when we are waiting for some input or output (such as a punch card or a magnetic tape).

Using this approach, we can develop unique queues: one queue for the time when we are on the computer and other queues for times when we are waiting for some input-output (I/O) device. We hope it will be possible to run all the jobs in parallel on the computer, so that we can keep the computer busy while one program is waiting for such an I/O device. Using this technique, we establish several queues: one for the computer and one for each of the I/O devices, such as a disc or drum, magnetic tape, card reader, or printer. Because only one program at a time can use these devices, there are potential queues for each of them. The waiting time in each of the queues is dependent upon two main factors: the individual job requirements, which we can assume are the same for all computers, and the hardware speed characteristics of the computer, which vary from one computer to another. It is important, then, that in our simulation we take these unique hardware characteristics into consideration. We can do this by scheduling events a variable amount of time in the future, instead of a fixed amount of time. The variables will be a function of the individual computer's characteristics.

The simulation of a communications network is closely related both to the simulation of a computer and to a simple network simulation. The basic problem in a digital communications network is one of storing information destined for some remote station, when that station is unavailable (perhaps because it is currently receiving information from another station). If the information must be stored and forwarded at a later time, a queue develops at the central switching center. We may wish to determine how much information will be stored during the worst traffic period, if, say, we are expected to switch 50 lines or stations, each with a unique traffic load. Here, as in the case of the computer simulation, we must determine the traffic patterns for each of the starting stations in order to develop a characteristic simulation.

These are just a few areas where simulation can be put to valuable use before making a sizable investment in plant and equipment. We have already shown that the computer costs can be negligible; in some cases, these costs will be under $50. The major cost will be to develop the program with a person experienced in the system to be simulated, and it is not necessary for him to be an experienced programmer. The object here is only to use the computer, not to master it; if the systems man is not familiar with higher-level computer languages, he can read a book on the subject or consult with the people at the service center for help in modeling his problem.

SECTION THREE

Inventory Control

There probably has been more literature written on inventory control techniques than on any other business planning technique. Most of it is extremely sophisticated, and little of it has attempted to solve the most basic problem—how we can design an inventory system for a computer that is inexpensive and is simple enough for an inventory manager or perhaps his secretary to use. This is what management wants—a system that its people, rather than a programmer, can control directly.

This section develops the basic systems requirements for such an inventory control system and discusses the hardware and software needed to implement such a system. It should be made clear at this point that our concern is with inventory from a production standpoint—that is, inventory in a manufacturing environment as opposed to a shop stockroom environment where items are stocked and withdrawn independently of other items in the inventory.

10

A Systems Design for Inventory

INVENTORY control is the orderly manipulation or control of the flow of inventory through a manufacturing shop. Because inventory itself has a cost, it is a variable that is subject to control. The object is to minimize the cost without penalizing the main production function. We can think of an inventory control system as a simulation of the real flow of inventory. The system serves two main purposes: First it allows us to learn more about the real flow of inventory, so that we can make certain judgments as to the maximum and minimum number of any given item that must be maintained in inventory; second, once we have determined the required parameters, the system allows us to control the actual flow so as to keep the inventory costs at a minimum.

There are many types of inventory control systems, and most of them have been in existence for more than a hundred years. As an example, the handling and saving of shipping and receiving bills is an elementary form of inventory control. The receiving bill usually goes to the front office, where it is recorded in a ledger book and an attempt is made to identify the current quantity of the item on hand.

We are all familiar with the yearly procedure of counting the number of parts on hand in a shop. This is an attempt to identify the current level of inventory and measure it in terms of dollars and cents. Each of these techniques is, in one form or another, an inventory control system; each in its own way is an attempt to measure or control the inventory within the shop. Although these are practical systems in certain situations, our concern here is with a much more sophisticated inventory system that will meet more of the requirements of a modern manufacturing operation.

Inventory Costs

It is important now to review inventory costs and determine the true cost of inventory so that we may appreciate how much money is tied up in the inventory function. Depending on how we slice the pie, there are a number of cost components in the inventory. For our purposes, let's arbitrarily break down the cost into four basic areas: item cost, hold cost, procurement cost, and shortage cost. It is possible to place all inventory costs in one of these four categories.

Item costs are usually quite straightforward, if we are considering outside procurement. If, however, we are considering doing our own manufacturing, which will be the case with some of our parts, the item cost becomes a much more complex variable. In this case there are three factors to consider: direct labor cost, direct material cost, and factory burden (which is a fixed rate applied to the direct labor costs). This seems simple enough. But direct labor costs are nonlinear variables; that is, the costs change in time on a given type of part. This is because of the so-called *learning curve*. For example, it takes less labor to build the second part than it does the first part, and still less to build the third part than the second part, because of increased manufacturing expertise.

The curve in Exhibit 10.1 demonstrates the concept of "manufacturing learning." The axis labeled "l" measures the amount of labor required to produce one unit of product, and the axis labeled "q" measures the quantity of product being produced. There are standard formulas for computing the curve in the figure.

The equation for determining item cost is:

$$IC = A \times R + M + A \times R \times B$$

where IC = item cost
A = average hours of labor per unit
R = hourly labor rate
M = material cost
B = burden rate

A can be replaced by the standard "learning" formula, if desired. The learning formula would make A a variable.

Another complication that should be considered in determining direct labor costs is that the rate at which improvement is made changes from

EXHIBIT 10.1

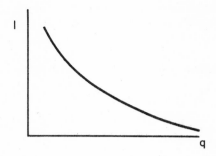

I = Amount of labor required to produce one unit of product.
q = Quantity of product being produced.

unit to unit, after a certain point decreasing in accordance with the principle of diminishing return. This is analogous to the total revenue curve in economics, which rises rapidly in low production quantities, levels off at some optimum quantity, and then actually begins to taper off.

Holding costs—the costs incurred to hold a part in inventory—include interest, storage, insurance, inventory administration, and taxes. Interest on inventory is usually computed as the "normal profit" on money, which every company adds to its fixed cost to arrive at the net fixed cost—between 5 and 20 percent. We can choose to identify normal profit with the current bank deposit interest, which is around 5 percent, or we may choose a higher figure, 8 to 9 percent, which the bank charges its customers. We may even choose a higher rate, comparable to our own return on assets.

Storage costs are those incurred for building space and maintenance. If you are renting space, a cost figure per square foot should be readily available. If you own space, the controller's office should have an equivalent figure, since space and maintenance costs are usually added on a rental basis—even though the building is the property of the manufacturer.

Inventory administration costs are those incurred for labor and materials in administering all the inventory. For example, the inventory monitoring and counting function and the inventory moving and dispatching function are included here. From these total costs, a per unit figure may be derived. This figure should then be included as part of the holding function. On the whole, these costs make up a substantial portion of the holding costs.

Procurement costs pertain to all costs incurred for processing orders. They are incurred mainly in the purchasing, accounting, and receiving departments, although additional costs will be incurred in the inspection, transportation, and internal handling of the products.

Shortage costs are usually difficult to calculate. What is the cost of delaying the shipment of a $500 product one month because some $2 part was unavailable when needed during the assembly period? Maybe four people sat idle for an hour because of the shortage, or maybe a customer was lost permanently or temporarily. Shortage costs are therefore not always easily defined, or evaluated, but we should keep them in mind when trying to determine the true cost of inventory.

In order to control all these costs properly so that we have an optimum balance between costs and manufacturing, we must be able to monitor and control the flow of inventory itself through the shop. At a minimum, for any kind of manufacturing shop this will require monitoring and controlling more than 2,000 parts or items of inventory, a task requiring an electronic computer and an inventory system or program.

Let us examine one possible inventory item in terms of its production components, and how we can relate these components to an inventory system. Let's begin at the top of the ladder and discuss what is called a top assembly item in the company. In a manufacturing company, this top assembly would be a deliverable product that has been assembled from other parts or subassemblies, which, in turn, have been made from lower-level assemblies. The various elements that go into making such a top assembly are illustrated diagramatically in Exhibit 10.2.

The top assembly, labeled item 482, is made up of three subassemblies: items 397, 465, and 888. Item 465 is actually the labor required to combine subassemblies 397 and 888 into the top assembly 482. Following item 397 down the tree, we find it is made up of two items (255 and 604), and some labor (262). Item 255 is made from parts 993 and 244 with no provision for labor, indicating that these two parts are probably procured from an outside source. Labor is treated as an item in inventory to allow for proper cost and scheduling analysis.

Functional Requirements of the System

The list that follows sets down a minimum set of requirements for a computer inventory system.

1. It must uniquely identify every item in the inventory by an item number, and maintain an item file in the memory space.

2. It must maintain the count for the current number of each item on

EXHIBIT 10.2

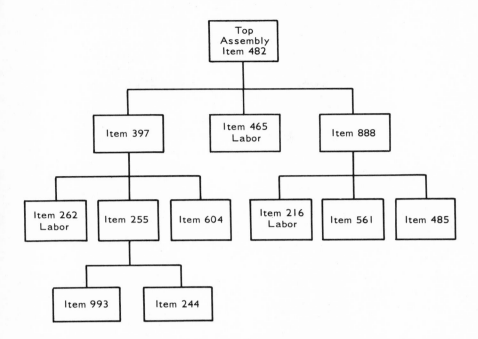

hand. This means that the system must recognize items received in and removed from inventory and must update the appropriate item files.

3. It must maintain the item cost in the item file.

4. It must compute the total dollar value of the inventory upon request. This is equivalent to multiplying the number on hand by the unit cost for each item and summarizing the value for the whole inventory.

5. It must compute and print out the dollar distribution of the inventory. This will also be expressed as a percentage of the total dollar value of the inventory.

6. It must produce a bill of materials for any item in the inventory. This means that each item in the inventory must have a pointer identifying the next higher and the next lower level of assembly, as in our manufacturing diagram in Exhibit 10.2. The pointers can be the item numbers of the next higher or next lower level of assembly.

7. It must identify all shortages in the inventory. A shortage can be identified by finding an item file which indicates that a certain quantity has been withdrawn, but a lesser quantity has been received at the next higher level of assembly. This capability is extremely helpful in auditing and monitoring the inventory.

8. It must monitor and record time in the system.

9. It must compute a dynamic demand rate for each item in the inventory. This can be used for projecting, forecasting, and determining the reorder level and quantity for each inventory item.

10. It must compute the true cost of any item in the inventory by summing the costs of all its related subassemblies. Whenever a new cost figure is entered into the file, the system must automatically recompute item costs for all related items that are at a higher level than the item in question.

11. It must handle labor as an item in inventory in the same way that it handles a part. Each item of labor will have a unit cost equal to the hourly rate multiplied by the quantity of hours required to assemble that level of part.

12. It must project past information into the future, so that minimum on-hand requirements for each item in inventory can be changed to reflect current demand.

13. It must print a list of all critical items in the inventory—that is, all items whose current on-hand supply is below the required minimum. The system might also produce the purchase orders for those items.

14. It must produce scheduling information concerning the time when any item in the inventory should be assembled.

15. It must compute labor requirements for each item in the inventory.

16. It must search the entire inventory file and identify all items which have become inactive. An inactive item is one that has not been received in or removed from inventory, or one that has no higher or lower level of assembly.

17. It must be able to add and delete entire items from the inventory. This also includes the requirement of being able to change an existing item.

Interface with the System

Our next step is to develop a system design for meeting these requirements and to provide for a human interface with the system that will be convenient and easy for the manufacturing people to use. Since the best inventory system in the world would be useless if the people who used it could not figure out how to enter data or get information out, the first rule is to make the system simple. We must bend the system to meet the user, not bend the user to meet the system.

First of all, let's follow the inventory flow through the shop so that we get an idea of how the system will behave and at what points we want a human interface with the computer. Normally, parts arrive at receiving, are checked in, and are placed into the inventory system. Here we must be able to tell the system what item was received, when it was received, and in what quantity. There are four pieces of information that we must input to the system: (1) the item number, (2) the fact that it was received rather than removed, (3) the quantity received, and (4) the date of receipt. These four pieces of information can be contained on a punch card.

Later, this same part will be removed from inventory and will be used, along with other parts, to develop the first level of assembly. The item will not be replaced in the inventory until a new part is received from the vendor. What will appear in the inventory, however, will be an item equal to the first level of assembly. Therefore, with the proper accounting procedures, the total dollar value of the inventory will not change because what is removed at a lower level is replaced at a higher level in the assembly process. During the time of assembly, however, the lower-level item must show up as a shortage. This will be helpful later in cost accounting and auditing.

In the removal process we again want to interface with the system to notify it that the part was removed from inventory so that it can decrease the quantity on hand and temporarily mark a shortage. In the removal process we convey four pieces of information to the system: (1) the item number, (2) the fact that an item was removed rather than received, (3) the quantity removed, and (4) the date of removal.

Next, we expect an item to be received into inventory as a replacement for the part that was used in assembly. Again we wish to interface with the system to increase the quantity of the item on hand by one and to eliminate the shortage that was posted when the lower-level item was removed from inventory. This procedure continues until the top-assembly item is shipped to the customer as a final product, at which time the item appears on the accounts receivable books.

In all these cases we find that punch cards have enough space to meet the input requirements of the system. This is not to imply, however, that we have the people in manufacturing entering data onto punch cards. The procedure here is to have them enter the data on 80-column coding sheets that have been preprinted with such labels as item number, quantity, and cost. These sheets can be passed along to the manufacturing people at the various logging points in the product flow and later given to a keypunch girl to enter on punch cards or magnetic tape. The forms are fairly simple and easy to adjust to, especially when the column labels are preprinted.

Time in an Inventory System

This brings us to a brief discussion of real time versus what we might call semireal time, and how they affect the inventory system. There are those who feel that in order to monitor and control the inventory properly, we must develop a real-time system, so that at the exact time a part is physically removed from inventory, the computer receives notice and updates the on-hand count for that part.

To achieve a real-time environment, however, is an extremely expensive proposition. First of all, it means that we must dedicate the computer to the system 100 percent of the time, even though there may not be a change in the system for long periods. Second it means that we must procure expensive remote-entry devices to be stationed at various possible change points in the system, so that the computer can be immediately notified of a system status change. This in turn forces us to provide expensive communications lines and multiplexing equipment, so that the computer can keep track of several remote-entry devices simultaneously.

Let us compare a real-time system with a semireal time system, with an eye to their potential relative costs. To begin with, the nature of inventory within a company is amenable to a semireal time schedule. During the lunch hours, coffee breaks, and evenings, the inventory does not change, and even if the actual on-hand count of a certain part is incorrect for several hours, chances are that nothing can be done about it during those periods.

We can therefore afford to enter all inventory changes into the system only once or twice per day. This can be done from a single entry point rather than several entry points by collecting the 80-column sheets from each of the stations, and having them keypunched onto cards or tape and entered into the computer at one station. Chances are that all the inventory changes can be read into the computer, and the files can be updated by the computer in less than 15 minutes. This would obviously represent a substantial saving over having the computer run for eight hours to do the inventory job. Before we make a decision to go with a real-time system, we must make certain therefore, that it is *absolutely* necessary.

Printouts from the Computer

In considering the output requirements for an inventory system, we should make it a rule to get printouts only when absolutely necessary. For example, we do not need a printout of the entire inventory file each evening. In fact, we do not really need a printout on an item until it is time to reorder. When printing out, we should get single copies and use a copy machine to reproduce that print. If we ask the computer operator to mount multiple copy paper in the printer, chances are he may have to abort the run, with all good intentions of returning to it later. But later he may not come back to it, and in the morning we will not have an inventory report. What is more, standard high-speed printer paper should be used for all inventory reports. There is no need to use special preprinted forms.

The Systems Design: Data Structure

We are ready now to begin a general design of the system. There are two basic parts to the system: a data structure and a program structure. The basic data structure for the inventory files takes up more than 90 percent of the storage space. Since the individual parts and items are the variables we wish to control, we delegate these files, each of which corresponds to an inventory part or item, to the storage space. The size of the files can vary. However, because it is much easier to program a fixed file length, we are using a fixed length for our problem.

We have set the fixed parameter to 100, which allows us up to 100 unique entries in the system. Each entry consists of 32 bits or 4 bytes of information, depending on whether we are working in the binary or alphanumeric system. In the list that follows, we assign specific values to each entry.

1–3.	Item number.
4.	Quantity on hand.
5.	Minimum quantity required on hand.
6.	Reorder quantity.
7.	Lead time in days.
8.	Item cost.
9.	Procurement cost.
10.	Holding cost.
11.	Shortage cost.
12.	Demand rate.
13.	Labor required for part.
14.	Labor rate in dollars.
15.	Maximum time to assemble part from lower level.
16–20.	Available for expansion.
21–40.	Alphanumeric description.
41–50.	Item number of next higher assembly.
51–60.	Item number of next lower assembly.
61–100.	Account number/quantity.

This particular layout is not the only one that can be used to set up the file; however, it is a good one because it is flexible. Notice that there is room for expansion from entry 16 to entry 20, if we decide to include more information about the item. We have left three entries open for item numbers, so we can have up to a 12-digit item number. If more items are required, we can set up some type of indexing scheme. Entries 1 through 40 are self-explanatory. Entries 41 through 50 are item numbers of related higher assemblies, and 51 through 60 are item numbers of related lower assemblies. Entries 61 through 100 are account numbers and quantities, which are used for accounting purposes to charge account numbers for parts removed from inventory.

The Systems Design: Program Structure

Our next concern is how to construct the internal data files for the most efficient manipulation of the data within the computer, as well as on the disc and the tape. We should plan to move as large a piece of data as possible in order to reduce the access time on the disc, reduce the interblock gaps on the tape, and keep the main storage requirements as small as possible. For this system, we move and work in blocks of 10 files at a time, and each file in our system requires 400 bytes, or characters; therefore, our block will be 4,000 bytes.

It is important to note that we will sometimes need as many as three working blocks of main storage at a time. This means that we must assign 12,000 bytes of main storage to data blocks. This storage will be used to move data blocks between punch cards, magnetic tape, and disc storage. When we actually start the job we will move the data onto the disc and work on it there. New information to update the data on the disc will come into the system from punch cards under the control of the program.

Exhibit 10.3 portrays the basic block structure of the data. The block has a rectangular structure 10 files wide and 100 words (4 bytes per word) deep. The 100 words contain the information about the items, as specified in our list of 100 entries.

The disc and the magnetic tape both carry data in blocks of an identical structure; therefore, as we bring data into main storage from the tape or disc, we bring it in as a rectangular block. Using a subscript technique, we can define the item numbers for each of the 10 files as $(1, 1)$, $(1, 2)$, $(1, 3)$ . . . $(1, 10)$, which would read from the left as row 1 column 1, row 1 column 2, row 1 column 3 . . . row 1 column 10. The data are also written out in a block fashion. If we had 2,000 items in inventory on a given day, we would have 200 blocks of data stored on tape when we complete the

EXHIBIT 10.3

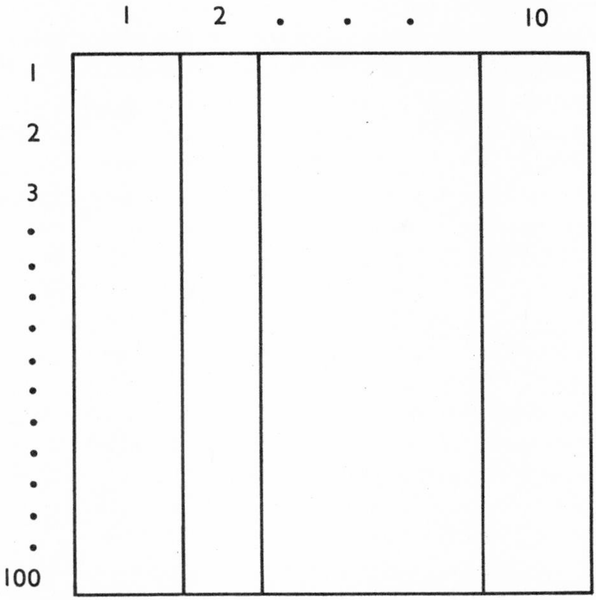

daily run. On the disc these data would take up 800,000 byte positions.

In addition to this block structure storage, we need space for the basic control program which will manipulate the data files. The control program is built around system MACRO commands. The commands themselves are of a general nature, so that the system has versatility but still provides a high-level, English type of interface to the user. This gives not only the programmer but also the manager and the secretary the opportunity to actually use the system.

Let us now consider the commands and how they work in the system. All the command cards are punched in columns 1–4 of a punch card, and the system automatically reads any card with a punch in any of those columns as a command card. All data cards associated with the commands are punched in columns 5–80.

1. LOAD. The LOAD command is used to tell the system that the inventory tape is mounted on the servo and that it should be read into memory and then written on the disc. The inventory records are kept on tape except when they are running, at which time they are moved onto the disc.

2. DUMP. The DUMP command is used to dump the disc onto tape. After completion of all updating runs, the up-to-date inventory file is copied onto tape.

3. ADD. The ADD command is used for adding new item files to the total inventory record or changing old ones. Data cards containing a relative location in a file and the value that is to be stored into the location follow this command card. As an example, we might find a card punched with the characters 5, 50. This tells the system to enter the value 50 in the fifth location of the specified item file, which in our item file corresponds to the minimum number of units required on hand.

4. DLTE. The DLTE command is used to delete files from the system. Following the command card will be cards containing the item numbers that are to be deleted from the main disc file.

5. RCVE. The RCVE command is used to notify the system about items or parts which were received into inventory since the last computer run. This command applies to all data cards following this one, until the next command card is reached. The format of the data cards is as follows: item number, quantity, date, account number. The system searches out the file identified by the item number, increases the number of parts on hand by the quantity named, and enters the date into the file. It then records the quantity and the account number in the space provided near the bottom of the file. This is used to develop a monthly corporate statement of the flow and cost of inventory during the month.

6. RMVE. The RMVE command is used to notify the system about all inventory removed since the last run. Data cards follow, and have a format similar to that of the RCVE command: item number, quantity, date, account number. The system handles these data in exactly the same fashion as it does the RCVE command, except it decreases rather than increases the number of parts on hand by the quantity specified.

7. CRTL. The CRTL command is used to make the system search all the item files and print out those files in which the current number of parts on hand is lower than the required minimum. This printed list can be used in determining when to reorder certain parts.

8. PRNT. The PRNT command is used to print out certain entries within each file. The format on the card might appear as: (1, 5) (10, 20). These two fields tell the system to print out the contents of locations 1–5 and then the contents of 10–20 for each file. In this fashion, the user can select only those entries in each file he is concerned with; he does not have to print out the entire file.

These eight commands that we have put into the system have to do strictly with the inventory function. Later we can add other commands to take advantage of all the accounting potential.

11

Implementation of the System on the Computer

In this chapter we'll explore the hardware and software requirements for the system, and discuss the actual implementation. Actually, we have already set down certain of these requirements in the preceding chapter. We decided to keep our total inventory file on magnetic tape in main storage, and to load the magnetic tape onto disc storage at the beginning of each run.

Once the file has been loaded onto the disc for updating the inventory, the disc is used exclusively. When the updating is complete and we are ready to terminate the computer run, we will tranfer the updated inventory files from the disc to magnetic tape. This basic manipulation and updating of the inventory will, of course, also require software. Let us explore each of these areas individually, so that we can have a better feel for both the cost and the schedule for such a job.

Magnetic tape, cards, and paper tape are called sequential devices, because they provide data to the system on a sequential basis. Such devices are not capable of providing data to the system in a short period of time. On a magnetic tape, for instance, the stored data can take several minutes to reach the program.

Magnetic tape is functionally the simplest device in the system; it is used for only one thing—to store data in a sequential fashion. Most tapes can perform five basic functions: read forward, read backward, write forward, backspace, and rewind to the beginning of tape. The tape itself is Mylar, about one-half inch wide and one-half mil thick, and usually has either seven or nine tracks. A track is a recording channel along the length of the tape, and pulses are recorded in each channel through one of seven or nine corresponding "write heads." The pulses, or bits, are represented as either a one or a zero, and are recorded on each channel in parallel. Each group of parallel bits has a unique pattern of ones and zeros, and is called a *character*. A character fills one frame on the tape.

Tapes usually have two characteristics which determine their data rate and capacity—tape speed and recording density. The recording density of the tape is usually expressed as the number of bits per inch along any one track. Because we are recording seven or nine bits (or one character) in parallel, we usually assume that the number of bits per inch is the same as the number of characters per inch. This number usually varies in the industry between 200 to 1,600. In fact, discrete values—200, 556, 800, or 1,600 bits per inch—have come about as industry standards.

A tape recorded at these densities should be compatible on any servo, but this is not always the case. Given the density, the tape speed therefore determines the instantaneous transfer rate of the servo, and tape speeds vary up to 200 inches per second, with an average of 100 inches per second. A tape that is recorded at 800 characters per inch will be capable of reading data at a rate of 80,000 characters per second. That is a lot of data in one second, even for the large, fast computers.

The recording mode on the tape is usually NRZI, which means non-return to zero change on ones. In order to have a compatible tape—one that any manufacturer can read—the tape must be written at one of the four densities mentioned earlier, and it must be written in NRZI. In this mode there is no change in the signal on the tape when there are zeros, and there *is* a change in signal when there are ones. The recording on the tape for a given pattern of ones and zeros is shown in Exhibit 11.1. Notice that the recording on the tape changes in polarity as a one is encountered;

EXHIBIT 11.1

Pattern   1   0   0   1   1   1   0   0   1   0   0   0   1

Tape

for zeros the polarity remains wherever it was. This technique of recording allows for a much greater density than RZ (or return to zero between bits).

Most tape servos have both a write head and a read head. The read head follows the write head by about one-half to three-quarters of an inch in the forward tape direction. Whenever the tape is writing, it is also reading back the recorded data to check for correct parity. This is normally called "read after write," and today it is standard on most tape servos. A parity check bit is recorded on the tape for each frame that is recorded. On a nine-channel tape, eight bits are used for data, and the servo itself generates the ninth bit as either a one or a zero, depending on whether the sum of ones in the first eight bits is odd or even. During tape reading, the hardware checks this parity bit to see if it is correct.

Most tape servos permit the writing of variable-length blocks on the tape. A block on tape is detected by an interblock gap. This is usually just over one-half inch (the same as the distance between the write head and the read head). This is necessary, since all data must be read back through the read head to check for correct parity. To do this it is necessary to continue moving the tape, even after a block is fully written, until all checking is complete. Some servos even provide logic for checking the vertical parity of a block on tape.

Most servos will handle 2,400-foot reels. After we discount two inches per foot for interblock gaps on the tape, there will be approximately 24,000 inches available for recording on tape. At 800 characters per inch, this means that the storage capacity of a tape is 19.2 million characters, which should be sufficient to contain files for up to 50,000 parts or items.

We can load the disc from tape in about four minutes, even if the tape is full. This seems to be a reasonable expenditure in time for such an inexpensive place to keep the inventory file. Keeping the files on a disc permanently would be a much more costly proposition. Each disc costs about $300 and holds about 2 million bytes; a tape costs $30 and holds up to 20 million bytes. Let us explore the disc in more detail and find out what its value is in the system, even though it costs more and holds less information.

The disc or drum is commonly known as a random access device and is usually used for intermediate storage of data which are frequently required by the system. The data on such a device are within a few milliseconds of the program. What was until recently called core memory, but is now referred to as main storage, is a random access device. Data in the main storage are only a few microseconds away from the program. In many cases, today, the number is down to nanoseconds; that is, parts of a microsecond.

Let us explore how data are actually recorded on the surface of a disc or drum. The surface is usually oxide or some type of metal plating, and flux or a magnetic field is recorded on this surface through a coil and a core. The recording mode varies among manufacturers and is the topic of heated debate among drum and disc engineers. The two main modes are RZ and NRZI, which we discussed briefly with respect to recording on tape.

In Exhibit 11.2 the term RZ refers to "return to zero," and the term NRZI refers to "nonreturn to zero change on ones." The difference between the two modes is that in RZ the pulse returns to the zero between the recording of any two sequential bits. In NRZI we change the recording pulse only when there is a one, and we never return to the zero condition. With today's modern ultra-high speed circuitry we usually get double the recording density using NRZI than we can get using RZ. The maximum practical recording density in the RZ mode today is about 700 bits per inch, as opposed to 1,500 bits per inch with NRZI. These figures do vary, however, depending upon the type of oxide or plating used.

One problem with NRZI is that we do not know whether the current bit being read is zero or one, unless we know what the bit before it was. This means that we must record a known starting pattern for blocks of data, so that the hardware can differentiate between a one and a zero as we get into the data. This means that in order to take advantage of the high recording density we must work on larger blocks of data, whereas with RZ we can (in theory) read or write a single bit at random.

The common feature of random access devices is an address. When the program requests data from such a device, it must give an address. For example, the program would be written to say "read the contents of disc location 1050 into main memory." The same applies to writing the disc. Core storage is the same. When we wish to load a register, we write "load register 3 with core storage location 605." If a drum or disc worked like a tape, we would be forced to take the next physical block of data on the disc or drum when doing a read. Since we can read or write from any place we want, however, it follows that we must name the place, and we do this with an address.

Address information, as well as data, is recorded on the surface of the disc or drum. The address information, however, cannot be written over; it can only be read from the surface. Every disc or drum has a clock track. This track is recorded at the density of the disc or drum and is continuously being read while the device is in operation. When a pulse comes off the clock track, the hardware knows that a data bit is currently over the read head, and a "gate" allows the bit through. When writing, the hardware knows that it can record the bit at this time.

EXHIBIT 11.2

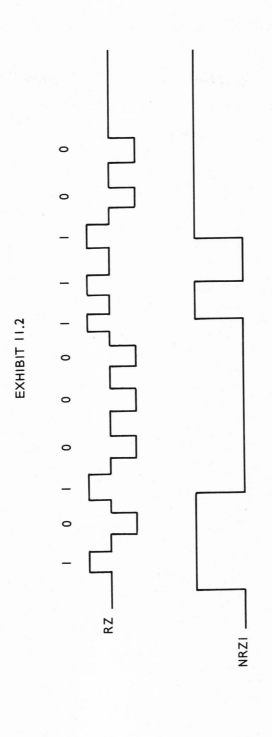

The disc and drum also have one track with a single pulse on it. This pulse corresponds to the beginning of the device or address zero. Many devices carry the addressing further than this. They designate a third track to carry one pulse for every eight pulses on the clock track; this tells the hardware that a byte has now passed by. Carrying the scheme still further, another track is used to mark word boundaries; for every 32 pulses on the clock track the word track has one pulse. Finally, a block track is also used. If the decision is made to record or read blocks of 256 words of 32 bits each, there will be one pulse on the block track for every 8,192 pulses on the clock. This system of tracks tells the hardware where it is on the device and enables it to find specific locations on the tracks.

Normally, then, address information is in two parts: One part gives the track address on the device; the other part gives the address of the information on that track. Most devices have several hundred tracks, with a minimum of 35 inches around the drum or disc per track. With 1,000 bits per inch, each track contains 35,000 bits, or 35,000/8 = 4,375 bytes or characters. If a disc, for example, has 200 tracks, it will have a capacity of close to 500,000 bytes on the disc surface. For our inventory control application, we have 2,000 items and we need roughly 400 bytes per item file, a total of 800,000 bytes. This means we need two discs or drums with a 500,000-byte capacity.

We still have not fully justified the expense of the disc or drum over tape. One of the chief advantages is the faster access time. Most random access devices of the rotor type turn at any of the following speeds: 900, 1,800, 3,600, and 7,200 revolutions per minute. We should allow for a slip of about 5 percent, but in theory we are never more than one revolution away from our data. On the average, we are exactly one-half of a revolution away; this is about 17 milliseconds away at 1,800 rpm. On most discs we must add 100 or so milliseconds to this time, to allow for moving the read/write head onto the correct track. On drums there is usually a head for each track, so there is no head motion time to be added on.

A drum or disc is usually more reliable than a tape, although there are exceptions. The failure rate on a drum or disc, in terms of dropping bits, is in the neighborhood of one bit dropped for every 10 billion bits that are transferred, and a reread usually picks up this one bit. There are reports that discs and drums can operate up to a year without a failure—tape has not been able to meet this performance. The initial cost of a disc or drum is usually much higher than the cost of a tape, but the disc or drum can save so much central computer time that it will actually save money in the end.

To set up and operate our inventory system, we need 64,000 bytes or 16,000 words of memory. Approximately 12,000 bytes or 3,000 words will be assigned to a supervisor or executive system that has a permanent residence in memory. This leaves 52,000 bytes or 13,000 words of 32 bits each. In this space we want to set aside as much room as possible for data storage, leaving only enough additional room for the main control program and the longest subprograms of the commands. Each command as described in the preceding chapter is a subprogram in the system. Each occupies a permanent position on the disc and is loaded into a common area in memory which is shared by each command. The main program calls in each subprogram as the command card is read from the card reader. The memory map should be similar to the layout shown in Exhibit 11.3.

In the layout, memory starts at location 0, the beginning of the supervisor program. Next we allocate a permanent area to data storage for the inventory problem. The main control program is stored next and requires approximately 1,000 words of memory. The common program overlay area space is used by the main program to load and unload subprograms from the disc as they are needed during the run. There is no need to keep these subprograms in memory when they are idle, thereby wasting valuable data storage space. The program overlay area must be equal to the longest subprogram that will occupy it—say, 5,000 words. This means that 7,000 words of memory are available for data storage. We will divide this up, assigning 2,000 words for a disc input buffer, 2,000 for a disc out-

EXHIBIT 11.3

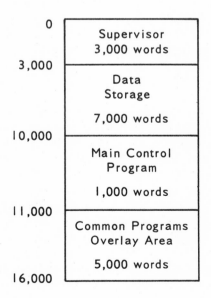

put buffer, 2,000 for a card or tape input or output buffer, and 1,000 for general working storage.

Let us now investigate how data will flow through this system. First of all let us examine the main program which will reside permanently in main storage. The program will be written in a higher-level language, preferably FORTRAN or COBOL, so that the program will have a reasonable chance of being compatible on several different types of computers. This program will automatically read cards from the card reader (or from tape, if there is no card reader) until it finds a card with a punch in column 1; this will be a command card. The command card causes the program to call the "system loader," which in turn loads the appropriate subprogram into the common memory. Once the subprogram is loaded, the main program transfers control to the subprogram.

Let us explore in some detail how such a subprogram might work by developing a basic design for the ADD command, as well as certain pertinent parts of the program and flow charts. The ADD command notifies the system that new item files are to be created or existing ones are to be changed. Following the command card are data cards telling it how to change the system. A typical sequence of such cards would be as follows:

1.	ADD		
2.	4073211		
3.		5	4000
4.		6	20000
5.	3921504		
6.		4	65
7.		5	10
8.		6	65
9.		7	8
10.		9	32.47

The first card contains ADD in columns 1–3 and causes the main program to load the subprogram ADD. The subprogram reads card 2, which says that item 4073211 either is to be added to the file or is already in the file and should be changed. Card 3 tells the system that entry 5 (the minimum on-hand quantity of the item) of the file should be changed to 4,000, and card 4 tells the system that entry 6 (the reorder quantity of the item) in the same file should be set to 20,000. Cards 5–10 tell the system what changes to make in the file for item 3921504.

If we have many item files that have to be changed, we can understand why we need a large card input buffer. If the card input buffer is 2,000 words, we have room for 8,000 bytes or 100 cards in the buffer. (Actually we can get considerably more into the buffer if we compress the data, but we'll take a simple course to start with.) Thus we can read 100 cards into the memory and sort all these cards (each of which will carry its respective data cards with it) in numerical order according to item numbers.

Once we have them sorted, we begin a pass through the disc files. Keep in mind that the item files on the disc are always kept in the same numerical order as the stack of cards in the card input buffer. Now we need only "do a merge"—that is, read the item file from low to high—until we find a match for the top item number in the card stack or until we find an item number in the disc stack that is larger than the top entry in the card stack.

Exhibit 11.4 shows a flow chart for this subprogram. This flow chart approaches the problem at a fairly high level, and it is a good policy to have a set of such charts available before the actual programming begins. If the programmer should leave, for example, the charts will serve as a good point of reference for a new trainee. Without them the trainee would have to begin studying the problem at the coding level, which can be extremely complex.

The general idea behind the design of this MACRO is to dedicate to a card buffer almost the entire data storage area, with the exception of 100 locations which will be used as a disc input buffer, so that we can read in as many cards as possible before starting a pass through the disc files. After we read in the cards we sort the buffer and merge the current disc files with the sorted card files, entering the combined files onto a new area of the disc.

The 16 steps of the flow chart in Exhibit 11.4 are numbered to enable us to follow the general flow. Steps 1, 2, and 3 are self-explanatory. At step 4 we begin an inner loop of the program. On the first pass through the program, we read in the first item file from the disc. (The second time we reach this point we read in the second file, and so on.) At step 5 we check to see whether the item meets the condition called for in that step—the condition that the item file number from the disc is lower than the item file number of the top card in the stack. If it is a lower number, we go to step 7, where we write the disc record back onto the disc at the new disc output area, after which we go back to step 4 and follow through on the next item.

However, if at step 5 the item file number from the disc is not a lower number than that of the top card in the stack, we go on to step 6 and check to see whether the disc item number is *equal* to the card item number. If the numbers are equal, we know that this is not a new item; it is an item that exists in our records but needs to be updated. In this case we go to step 8 and change the current disc record.

EXHIBIT II.4

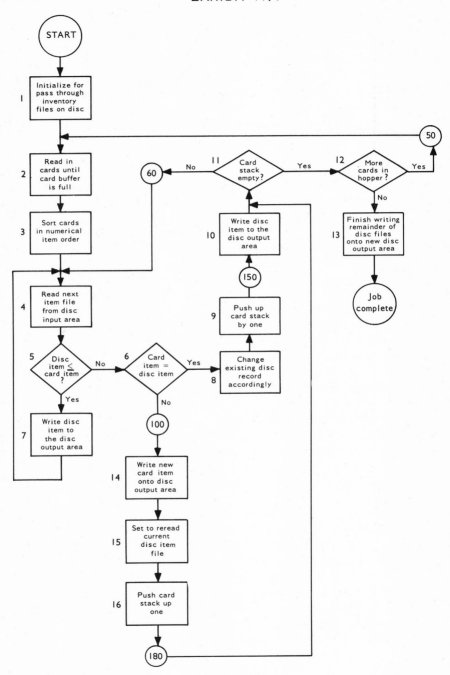

Following the 8–9 leg of the chart, we move on to step 9, where we push the card stack up one position, since we have eliminated the top card in the stack, and then move through 150 to step 10. Here we write the updated disc record onto the disc output area, in its sequential position behind the other records. At step 11 we test to find out whether the card stack is empty. If it is not empty, we go to 60, which leads us back to step 4 where we repeat the process with a new item file. However, if it is empty we move to step 12, where we examine the card hopper to see whether there are more cards for the ADD command. If there are more cards we go to 50, which takes us back to step 2 of the program, where we begin again. If there are no more cards in the hopper we go to step 13, where we continue to read the records of the remaining item files from the old disc area and rewrite them in the new disc area. At this point we have a complete, sorted string of the inventory files on the new disc output area, and the job is complete.

We must move backward to step 6 at this point, in order to follow the alternate leg through the chart. If the disc item number and the card item number are not equal, we have a new item that belongs on the disc at this point in the sequence. At step 14 we write the new card item onto the disc and move to step 15, where we set to reread the current disc item file from where we stopped. At step 16 we push the card stack up one position, thereby eliminating the top entry. We move through 180 to step 11, which is the check to see whether the card stack is empty. This completes the description of all the steps and paths in the chart; eventually we have to end up at step 13, regardless of which paths we have followed, and the JOB COMPLETE stage will notify us that we have completed the ADD command.

With the exception of steps 3 and 13, all steps in the flow chart can be accomplished in fewer than five FORTRAN statements. Step 9, for example, can be written in two simple statements:

$$DO \; 100 \; I = 1, 1980$$
$$100 \; KCARD(I) = KCARD(I + 20)$$

We decided to have 2,000 words of memory for a card buffer, which is reserved for the array named KCARD. Each punch card takes 80 bytes of memory, and each word has 4 bytes; therefore, each card takes up 20 words. Recall that a DO statement causes the compiler to repeat all instructions down to 100. Each time the statement is repeated, the variable I, whose value will vary from 1 to 1980, is increased by one. When the value $I = 1980$, the compiler will stop doing the instruction and step down to the next instruction. These two statements cause the computer to move the 21st entry up to the first entry, the 22nd entry up to the 2nd entry, and so forth. In this fashion the top card (or in effect the top 20 words of the stack) is eliminated, and all remaining cards are one higher in the stack.

Step 5, which checks to see whether the disc item number is lower than the card item number, is written in one statement as follows:

$$\text{IF } [\text{KDSC (I)} - \text{KCARD (I)}]\ 7, 6, 6$$

In this case, the part of the statement within the parentheses is computed by the compiler, and, depending on whether the result is negative, zero, or positive, the compiler goes to statement 7 or 6. In this example KDSC is the disc input buffer which contains the next record from the disc file. These alphanumeric item numbers can be treated as purely numerical values in FORTRAN without loss of the proper sorting relationship. If the expression is negative, the item number from the disc record is lower than the item number from the card record, in which case we go to step 7. If the two values are equal, we get a zero result from the question, and we go to step 6. If the disc item number is higher than the card item number, the result is positive, and we also go to step 6.

These, of course, are isolated statements that must be supported by some "housekeeping" statements, but they should serve to show the simplicity of implementation. We should be able to implement this subprogram with fewer than 100 FORTRAN statements, and it should not take us much more than a week to flow-chart, document, code, and debug this particular subprogram. This estimate includes a user document that will explain how to punch the input cards and tell us what the results will be. We should have a total of approximately 20 basic commands, 7 of which we have already described. The ADD command is one of the most difficult. It is fair to say, then, that 20 weeks would be a decent period of time in which to implement the total inventory package. Even if we double the time estimate to 40 weeks, our inventory control system will still be set up in less than a year, a reasonable expenditure of time for this expensive effort.

Today there are many computer service centers that have or can develop inventory systems. But the user should be on his toes; these systems often offer too much of what is not needed and scarcely anything of what is needed. The problem often lies in the fact that the service center does not correctly or fully understand a company's specific problem.

If we decide to have a service center develop a system, we should ask each service that bids for the contract to develop the package in a higher-level language and to include the following information in its presentation:

1. A general write-up of each MACRO. (It is important that we, the users, be able to understand these commands.)

2. A network schedule that will tell us how long it will take to develop each MACRO.

In this chapter, the description of the hardware and software requirements for an inventory control system was by no means complete, and it was not intended to be followed as a guide for setting up a system within any specific company. However, in conjunction with the description of a general systems design it *was* intended to give us an idea of how we can implement a relatively simple and inexpensive system. If we keep these general guidelines in mind when we plan an inventory control system, we can help insure that our system will fulfill our needs rather than present us with a new business problem in the form of the computer itself.

Linear Programming

This last section deals with linear programming—a technique used to determine which of several alternative courses of action offers the optimum plan. It is without question one of the most complex yet potentially one of the most useful planning techniques in business today. Much has been written about linear programming over the past 20 years, but most of this literature is highly theoretical and therefore appeals to a limited group of professionals. Although the science is a tool for management use in decision making, the literature is aimed at mathematicians. The next few chapters develop some of the concepts of linear programming through a simplified solution technique, which can be explained largely without mathematics beyond simple arithmetic.

Linear programming is being used today in just about every industry. It is a tool for scheduling production, for market forecasting, and for controlling plant operation. There is no business area where the science has not been put to use since its inception in the 1940s. Today for every production type of linear programming model there are ten research models, and each year management accepts one or two more of these research models into the production group. This is a science that is growing by leaps and bounds, and each of us will eventually encounter a problem that this technique can help solve. It is wise, then, to develop a working knowledge of the subject so that we can recognize a problem that can be solved with linear programming.

12

The Linear Programming Technique

SINCE linear programming has to do with alternatives, we may well ask, "What are the alternatives?" Basically, they are different ways and means of doing things. For instance, there are several ways of shipping a product from one point to another: by air, by rail, or by truck. We also have a choice of routes for each means of transportation, and if we add a second product we have twice as many alternatives. It doesn't take many variables in a problem to have literally thousands of alternatives, and once the alternatives reach this level it is next to impossible to resolve each one independently.

For example, there are more than 3.5 million ways to assign ten men to ten different jobs. Let's assume that each man can perform each job with a varying degree of efficiency, in terms of the time it takes to do each job. We want to assign the jobs in such a way that a minimum amount of time is consumed in completing all the work. Obviously it would be impossible to resolve each alternative individually—or would it? With linear programming there exists a method by which each alternative can at least be taken

Note: Chapters 12 and 13 are adapted in part from James P. Fourre, *Understanding Linear Programming*, AMA Management Bulletin 94, 1967.

into consideration. This does not mean that every possible alternative is calculated and compared with all others until the best one is found.

With linear programming, we start with any feasible solution. We move from that solution to a better one, using a somewhat magical technique, until the technique cannot find a better solution. The technique is such that when we reach a stage where it cannot find a better solution than the current one, we know there *are* no better solutions.

Why should we complain when each iteration improves on the solution before it? We shouldn't really care if the iterations go on forever. However, they don't go on forever. Because there is a finite number of alternatives, there must be a finite number of iterations—given that each iteration produces a new unique alternative. Best of all, with each iteration we skip over many alternatives which are not as good as the new one. Those alternatives will never again have to be considered in the problem. We can see how this technique works by examining Exhibit 12.1.

EXHIBIT 12.1

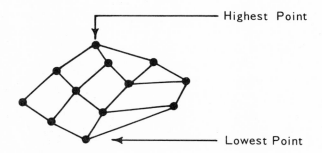

The relative vertical positions of the dots are the key points. In Exhibit 12.1 the dot labeled "highest point" is higher on the page than the other dots, and the dot labeled "lowest point" is lower on the page than the other dots. There is a lower point from every point in the figure except, obviously, from the very lowest; in linear programming this lowest point is called the *optimum, maximum, minimum,* or *best* alternative.

If we think of the dots as alternatives, Exhibit 12.1 is analogous to a linear programming problem. From any point in the figure we can move to any one of several adjacent points. Notice, however, that we cannot move to all the points in the figure from any one point without making several steps through other points. The magical technique helps us move to a *better* point with each step.

At this point, let's outline the three basic steps essential to the formulation of a problem for a linear program:

1. Define all alternatives.
2. Compute a single value, the "objective" value, for each alternative.
3. From among the objective values, pick either the minimum or the maximum value. We will call this the optimum value.

Each of these steps must be performed in order to find the optimum solution to a multialternative problem. Each step would make sense if we were doing a straightforward hand computation of the problem. We know, for instance, that before we can find the best or optimum alternative, we must first define all the alternatives, as in step 1. Second, we must formulate what we mean by the optimum, which, in linear programming, is always a single value, either maximum or minimum. So, as in step 2, we must formulate an objective function which turns each alternative into a single value. Step 3 is fairly straightforward; we pick from among all possible objective values either a maximum or minimum.

We have already determined that a one-at-a-time approach which examines each alternative would be out of the question. Even on a high-speed digital computer the simplest problem would be too costly and time-consuming; in the case of ten men on ten jobs, over 30 million computations would be required. If we had a hundred men on a hundred jobs, trillions of computations would have to be made. We do need some magic in our technique to aid us in reducing the computational load. The magical technique is what linear programming is all about—it provides a way to cope with problems that are otherwise impossible from a computational standpoint.

The technique as used in the transportation industry is called the transportation algorithm, but it works only on simple problems. A more sophisticated method, called the simplex technique, is employed in other areas. This involves solving a set of linear equations simultaneously, as is shown in some detail in a later chapter.

The best way to demonstrate the concepts employed in linear programming is to show how the technique can be used to solve a common business problem. Linear programming has many applications in the transportation field, especially as a tool for minimizing shipping costs between several factories and several warehouses. This type of problem breaks down into one of scheduling goods to be shipped from factories with limited capacity to warehouses jobbers, or the final retail outlets at minimum cost. It is assumed that the warehouses have a known demand, which is derived from sales forecasts or from minimum inventory requirements that must be maintained. Clearly, such a situation presents many alternatives which tend to increase geometrically as the number of factories and warehouses increases arithmetically.

Even with relatively few factories and warehouses, the eyeball method of solution soon becomes impractical. For example, in the case of three factories and three warehouses, there are nine possible ways to ship to the warehouses—three from each factory. This solution assumes that only one factory can supply a warehouse; if we disregard this restriction and allow for fractional shipments, the number of possible solutions is infinitely greater.

Our problem is to develop a schedule or program that meets demand at the warehouses without exceeding factory capacity, and to accomplish this at a minimum cost in transportation. It is assumed here that the shipping costs are known between every factory and every warehouse. An equivalent problem would be to minimize the shipping time, in which case time between points would replace the cost data.

Let us examine a specific application. Assume that a manufacturer of automobile tires was considering replenishing inventories at his key warehouses, which were strategically located within so-called marketing regions around the nation. The warehouses, in turn, supplied jobbers who met current consumer demand. This particular manufacturer divided the nation into four marketing regions, each with a warehouse as a central supply point for jobbers. Construction of factories at the strategic marketing points to save transportation and storage costs had been considered, but this idea was dropped because it was found that factory operating costs were usually higher at these locations.

Warehouse demand was submitted by tire size and quantity, and freight costs were available in terms of weight. Obviously, there would be a quantity difference between 1,000 pounds of tires of one size and 1,000 pounds of another size, and the initial conclusion was that several independent scheduling problems had to be solved. In fact, there were as many independent problems as there were different tire sizes.

After more careful consideration, it was decided that the costs involved in solving several independent problems would exceed any losses incurred by averaging out the tire weights and considering the tires as a uniform product. It was decided that the shipping schedule obtained by an average would be close enough to the optimum schedule, because the sales forecasts themselves were only estimates with an error factor of up to 10 percent. Finally, a decision was made to standardize the computations on the basis of 100 pounds, since this was the unit of account used by the various carriers.

Data concerning the shipping costs of carriers, the demand requirements of warehouses, and the known factory capacities for a three-month period were accumulated and arranged as shown in Exhibit 12.2. Shipping cost from factory one (F1) to warehouse two (W2) is $7 per 100

EXHIBIT 12.2

Cost per 100 lbs.

	W1	W2	W3	W4	Capacity
F1	6	7	17	21	600
F2	17	4	10	12	900
F3	22	8	5	4	700
F4	12	4	11	6	800
Demand	800	800	900	500	

pounds. The cost for shipping 100 pounds from factory three (F3) to warehouse three (W3) is $5. The table also shows each factory's maximum capacity in the right-hand column; for example, factory two (F2) has a maximum capacity of nine hundred 100-pound groups of tires during the three-month period. The bottom row of the table shows the warehouse demand. Warehouse two (W2), for example, needs eight hundred 100-pound groups of tires during the period.

We now have sufficient data to compute an optimum shipping schedule. Before we do, however, notice that the sum of the factory capacities equals the sum of the warehouse demands. In any transportation problem, unless the supply is at least as large as the demand, there is no feasible solution.

A more practical set of factory capacities would have been one whose sum was greater than the warehouse demands—it is a rare situation when the total current market demand equals total factory capacity. These values have been picked to cut down on the amount of computation.

We start by finding any feasible solution to the problem. Using cost data, we evaluate changes to the initial solution in an effort to derive a better one. We then evaluate this solution to see whether improvement can be made. When evaluation shows that no improvement can be made, we stop—we now have the optimum solution.

Exhibit 12.3, which shows the first feasible solution, is developed by the so-called northwest corner rule. We start in the northwest corner of the table—factory one (F1), warehouse one (W1). In this square we enter the smaller of two values: either the warehouse demand for W1 or the factory capacity for F1. In this particular case the warehouse demand is 800 units and the factory capacity is only 600 units; so we enter 600 in the square. This will be the amount shipped from factory one to warehouse one. Note that this does not completely satisfy the demand at W1, but it is the maximum amount that could be shipped from F1 to W1 because it exhausts the factory's capacity.

The next step, since we have not yet satisfied the total demand, is to move down the first column to square F2-W1, where we enter the smaller of either factory capacity for F2 or warehouse demand for W1. The warehouse demand at W1 is 200 units, because we have already supplied 600 units of a total of 800 required from the square above, and the factory capacity for F2 is 900 units. The smaller value is 200; so we enter it in square F2-W1. At this point we have satisfied all requirements at W1 without exceeding the capacity of F1 and F2. In fact, F2 still has 700 units of capacity.

EXHIBIT 12.3

	W1	W2	W3	W4	Capacity
F1	6 (600)	7	17	21	600
F2	17 (200)	4 (700)	10	12	900
F3	22	8 (100)	5 (600)	4	700
F4	12	4	11 (300)	6 (500)	800
Demand	800	800	900	500	

When we have completed a column—a warehouse demand—we move to the next column on the right and repeat the process. Because there is no capacity remaining at F1, we must start in the row labeled F2, which has 900 units of total capacity, of which 200 units have already been used. We enter, then, in square F2-W2, the smaller of either the warehouse demand for W2 or the factory capacity for F2. W2 demand is 800 units and F2 capacity is now 700 units; therefore, we enter 700 in square F2-W2. We have now used all capacity for F1 and F2 and have met all requirements at W1. However, we still must supply W2 with 100 units, so we move down one square in the column labeled W2, check for the smaller value, which is 100, and enter it in the square.

At this point we have satisfied the requirements at both W1 and W2, we have exhausted the total capacity at F1 and F2, and we have used 100 units of the capacity at F3. Moving to square F3-W3, we enter 600, the smaller of demand at W3 (900 units) and the remaining capacity at F3 (600 units). We continue satisfying the demand at W3 by entering 300 in square F4-W3. We are then left with 500 units of capacity at F4, which satisfies exactly the requirements at W4. This will always be the case when the total capacity at all the factories is equal to the total demand at all the warehouses.

The completed table represents a feasible solution to the problem. All warehouse demands are met within the available factory capacity. Note that the sum of the entries across a row equals the factory capacity for that row, and the sum of the entries down a column equals the warehouse demand for that column. For example, W3 requires 900 units; 600 units come from F3, and 300 units come from F4.

This table will be used in stepping from one solution to another. With each step, the size of the numbers in the table will change and they will occupy different squares. We can, without any loss of generality, assume that every square in the table has a numerical value, and if a square has no entry, this value is zero. As the numbers in the squares are changed to form new solutions, we must always make sure that the sum across any row is equal to the factory capacity for that row, and the sum down any column is equal to the requirements at the warehouse for that column. If these conditions are met, and only if these conditions are met, will we have a feasible solution.

The solution shown in Exhibit 12.3 has an associated total cost. This cost can be obtained by multiplying the individual costs—entered in the upper left-hand corner of each square—by the value of the quantity in that square. (If the square has no quantity entry we of course ignore that square.) The computation is as follows: $(6 \times 600) + (17 \times 200) + (4 \times 700) + (8 \times 100) + (5 \times 600) + (11 \times 300) + (6 \times 500) =$

$19,900. The first term (6×600) is taken from square F1-W1 of the exhibit, and the other terms are developed in a similar fashion from the other squares.

As a next step in the transportation technique, let us examine a procedure for moving from one solution to another. If we arbitrarily decide to move the first 600 units from F1 to W2 instead of to W1, we move 600 units from square F1-W1 across to square F1-W2. The arrow in the first row of Exhibit 12.4 shows the direction of the move. This situation is feasible with respect to the factory capacity, because this move causes square F1-W1 to go to zero, and the sum of the elements in the first row is still 600. But if we make this move without any other adjustments, demand at W1 and W2 will be out of balance—these columns will not add up to their required amounts. To offset this deficiency we must take 600 units from square F2-W2 and move them to the left to square F2-W1. This move is also indicated by an arrow. This brings the first and second columns into balance without disturbing the sum in the second row. These two moves, as indicated by the arrows, will give us a new feasible solution (Exhibit 12.5).

All rows add up to their corresponding entry in the right-hand col-

EXHIBIT 12.4

	W 1	W 2	W 3	W 4	
F 1	6 — 600 →	7	17	21	600
F 2	17 — 200 ←	4 — 700	10	12	900
F 3	22	8 — 100	5 — 600	4	700
F 4	12	4	11 — 300	6 — 500	800
	800	800	900	500	

EXHIBIT 12.5

	W1	W2	W3	W4	
F1	6	7 (600)	17	21	600
F2	17 (800)	4 (100)	10	12	900
F3	22	8 (100)	5 (600)	4	700
F4	12	4	11 (300)	6 (500)	800
	800	800	900	500	

umn, and all columns add up to their corresponding entry in the bottom row. Under the new schedule shown in Exhibit 12.5, we ship 600 units to warehouse two from factory one. To offset this we no longer ship anything from factory one to warehouse one. In order to meet the demand requirements of warehouse one, we assign 600 additional units from factory two. The total cost is calculated as follows: $(7 \times 600) + (17 \times 800) + (4 \times 100) + (8 \times 100) + (5 \times 600) + (11 \times 300) + (6 \times 500) = $28,300$. This is certainly not a better solution—it costs us $8,400 more than the first. We could continue in this fashion, picking other alternatives at random and computing the costs for each until we find the optimum, but this is unnecessary.

We are now in a position to develop a technique for evaluating each solution and for finding a better one if it exists. In the move from the first to the second solution, only four squares were involved. By evaluating the cost in the squares before making the move from one solution to the next, we can actually determine whether the move will increase or decrease the total cost. If we see that it increases the total cost, we can avoid the move completely.

As an example, for each unit that we take out of square F1-W1, total costs are reduced by $6, and for each unit moved into square F1-W2, total costs are increased by $7. The net effect of moving a unit from square F1-W1 to F1-W2 is to increase total cost by $1, so the total effect of the move in row one is an increase in cost of $600. In addition, we must evaluate the net effect of restoring the balance by shifting 600 units from W2 to W1 in the second row. For each unit that we take out of square F2-W2, the total cost is reduced by $4, and for each unit moved into square F2-W1, the total cost is increased by $17, so the net effect of this move is a $13 increase in total cost for each unit moved. In other words, net change equals $17 minus $4. The net change in total cost by this move for 600 units is $7,800.

Considering the net effect of both moves, we add as follows: $7,800 + $600 = $8,400—our difference in total cost between the two solutions. If we add this figure to the total cost for the first solution, we get $28,300— the cost of the second solution. If we had known this in the first place, we would never have made the move.

The procedure after reaching the first solution is to perform a cost evaluation, similar to that just completed, for each empty square in the table on a unit basis. In our example the total net effect of moving one unit was $14, and this value had four basic components:

1. The cost in square F1-W2.
2. The cost in square F1-W1.
3. The cost in square F2-W1.
4. The cost in square F2-W2.

Because we are moving units into squares F1-W2 and F2-W1, items 1 and 3 contribute positively to the net effect. And because we are moving units out of squares F1-W1 and F2-W2, items 2 and 4 contribute negatively to the net effect. The final computation is as follows: $7 — $6 + $17 — $4 = $14.

Notice that the procedure involves one vacant square and then a series of occupied squares that basically close a loop. The rules governing this procedure have not been established arbitrarily; they are consistent with the mathematics of the problem. They can be resolved, however, by pure reason as they were in the first case.

Let us evaluate square F1-W3 from Exhibit 12.6. The loop to be used is indicated by arrows. If we move a unit from square F3-W3 to F1-W3, we find that the first and third rows are out of balance. To restore the balance to the third row, we must move one unit from square F2-W2 to square F3-W2. Now, however, the first and second rows are out of balance. We offset this by moving one unit from square F1-W1 to square F2-W1, which completes the loop.

146

The value 27 entered in square F1-W3 is the evaluation coefficient for the square. It is derived from the costs in the squares forming the loop similar to our first case. If we use the head of the arrow to indicate a positive contribution to the net costs, and the tail to indicate a negative contribution, we get the following for the three arrows: $17 — $5 + $8 — $4 + $17 — $6 = $27. This indicates that for each unit we move around the loop indicated by the arrows, the total costs will go up by $27. Immediately we know that this move, at least for the present, is out of the question.

Establishing a loop with this procedure is basically a trial-and-error technique. The loop obviously must be completed to restore the balance. If we take something out of a particular row or column, that row or column will be short and must be replenished from another row or column, which then will be short. This shortage must, in turn, be supplied from another row or column. The process is continued until we come back to the row or column that received units at the start. Because this row or column has an oversupply, it can be used to restore the balance in the shorted row or column just preceding it.

Note that in the example just completed, we can move around the loop

EXHIBIT 12.6

	W1	W2	W3	W4	
F1	6 / 600	7 / 14	17 / 27	21 /	600
F2	17 / 200	4 / 700	10 /	12 /	900
F3	22 /	8 / 100	5 / 600	4 /	700
F4	12 /	4 /	11 / 300	6 / 500	800
	800	800	900	500	

in the opposite direction as indicated by the arrows in Exhibit 12.7. The evaluation coefficient is still the same if we complete the loop in the opposite direction; that is, $17 - \$6 + \$17 - \$4 + \$8 - \$5 = \$27$. Again, as in the previous case, the loop involves one empty or zero square and a series of occupied squares.

This type of loop is called a simple loop. For every empty square in the table, one and only one such loop exists. This means that we can compute an evaluation coefficient for each empty square in the table and that the coefficient will be unique. These data are entered into the empty squares of Exhibit 12.7 as in the first two cases. The evaluation coefficients in the table show that with the exception of two squares, all other moves will increase the total cost. The two squares which will improve the total costs are F4-W1 and F4-W2. Each of these squares has a negative evaluation coefficient. We pick the square which will reduce the cost by the greatest amount for each unit moved—that is, square F4-W1.

An important concept at this point, which can be proved in the mathematics, is that at the optimum solution no more than seven squares will be nonzero. For the general case, if there are M rows and N columns in the

EXHIBIT 12.7

	W1	W2	W3	W4	
F1	6 (600)	7 14	17 27	21 36	600
F2	17 (200)	4 (700)	10 9	12 16	900
F3	22 1	8 (100)	5 (600)	4 4	700
F4	12 −15	4 −10	11 (300)	6 (500)	800
	800	800	900	500	

EXHIBIT 12.8

	W1	W2	W3	W4	
F1	6 (600)	7 24	17 12	21 21	600
F2	17 (100)	4 (800)	10 −6	12 1	900
F3	22 16	8 15	5 (700)	4 4	700
F4	12 (100)	4 5	11 (200)	6 (500)	800
	800	800	900	500	

problem, no more than M + N — 1 squares will be nonzero at the optimum solution. For our case, then, we know that we will reach an optimum with no more than seven squares occupied.

Our objective, once we have determined which square we should move units into, should be to move units into the square from around the loop until one of the squares around the loop reaches zero. Although we know that for each unit we move into an unoccupied square with a negative cost coefficient we reduce the cost by the amount of the coefficient, we cannot move any more units than we have available. If we did move more than were available, we would get negative numbers in the loop, which would make no sense. With this procedure, then, we make a new occupied square and eliminate an old one, thus maintaining seven occupied squares.

Let us start by making the first move into square F4-W1. We will move in the loop as follows: from F2-W1 to F4-W1; from F3-W2 to F2-W2; and from F4-W3 to F3-W3. The minimum amount in the squares in this loop is 100 units. This is in square F3-W2. After we have moved 100 units around the loop into square F4-W1, the square F3-W2 will become zero. At this point we must stop. The new solution appears in Exhibit 12.8.

As a check against the computational work, we insure that the sum of each row adds up to the corresponding entry in the right-hand column; and the sums down the columns add up to the corresponding entry in the bottom row. This then completes the first move. It represents a feasible solution whose total costs are less than the first feasible solution; thus the second solution is better than the first. We now recompute the evaluation costs for the empty squares and enter them as shown in Exhibit 12.8.

We find from the evaluation coefficients that square F2-W3 is the only move which will reduce costs. The loop for the move is as follows: from F4-W3 to F2-W3 and from F2-W1 to F4-W1. The minimum amount in the loop is 100; so we move 100 units around the loop. This causes square F2-W1 to go to zero. The new solution is shown in Exhibit 12.9.

EXHIBIT 12.9

	W1	W2	W3	W4	
F1	6 (600)	7 / 8	17 / 12	21 / 21	600
F2	17 / 6	4 (800)	10 (100)	12 / 7	900
F3	22 / 16	8 / 9	5 (700)	4 / 4	700
F4	12 (200)	4 / −1	11 (100)	6 (500)	800
	800	800	900	500	

If there are any negative coefficients, we choose the largest and move to a new schedule in similar fashion to the method just demonstrated. We continue this process until all squares show a positive or zero evaluation coefficient. At this point we will have reached an optimum because any move from this schedule will only increase total costs. If we were to repeat this process until we reached an optimum solution, we would get the following shipping schedule:

Ship 600 units from F1 to W1.
Ship 700 units from F2 to W2.
Ship 200 units from F2 to W3.
Ship 700 units from F3 to W3.
Ship 200 units from F4 to W1.
Ship 100 units from F4 to W2.
Ship 500 units from F4 to W4.

The schedule (see Exhibit 12.10) is feasible because it meets all the requirements at both factories and warehouses. One of the advantages of this technique is that the final schedule can stand by itself unsupported by any previous work. Even if we had made a mistake in earlier work and arrived at the table in Exhibit 12.10 through faulty computations, it tells us that this is a feasible solution—one that meets the problem requirements and cannot be improved upon because all evaluation coefficients are positive. This is really all that we were after in the first place—that is,

EXHIBIT 12.10

	W1		W2		W3		W4		
F1	6		7		17		21		
		(600)		9		13		21	600
F2	17		4		10		12		
		5		(700)		(200)		6	900
F3	22		8		5		4		
		5		9		(700)		3	700
F4	12		4		11		6		
		(200)		(100)		1		(500)	800
		800		800		900		500	

the minimum cost schedule, which in this case is $17,700 for our three-month period.

How could we handle this problem if the warehouse demand exceeded the factory capacity for the period? The basic approach to this problem is to consider overtime in terms of a second shift. This would, in effect, double the total capacity. In this situation, however, there are special cost considerations which now must be included in the problem; for example, operating costs between shifts may vary substantially. In our first problem we did not consider the production cost at the factories, because this figure was assumed to be about the same for each factory; consequently, it would not be a determining factor in the minimum cost. But if we go into second shifts and overtime there is an additional dimension to the problem.

Let us consider both production and transportation simultaneously. If we considered the transportation problem independently of the production costs, we would probably find that we had excess capacity available in every factory; therefore, we would ship all units required by a warehouse from the factory with the cheapest shipping costs. This would force some factories to work overtime while others would not be working a full shift. This certainly minimizes transportation costs but is inefficient from a production cost standpoint.

This problem can be handled with two simple extensions to the original problem. First, we consider each factory as two factories—one for the first shift and one for the second shift—or a total of eight factories. Second, we add the cost of production at each of the eight factories to the transportation cost. Naturally, the second-shift factories will have a greater production cost.

We assume that the transportation cost between a warehouse and a prime-shift factory and its associated second-shift factory are the same. Production costs, then, must be established on the same basis as the transportation costs—that is, on 100-pound units. These costs should include only variable costs. Costs that must be incurred regardless of production levels should be excluded. The problem can be set up in tabular form similar to that used for the first problem. The table for this problem will have eight rows—one for each factory—instead of four as in the original problem; and it will have four columns, one for each warehouse. The solution technique will be the same as in the original problem.

In this new formulation of the problem we are actually solving two problems simultaneously—one in transportation and one in production. If we were to drop the transportation portion, we would be solving a problem purely in production, which leads us to the conclusion that the transportation technique can be used to solve many different types of problems. In addition to a wide range of applications, the technique enjoys an additional advantage over the purely mathematical formulation of the problem in that fairly sizable problems can be solved with only pencil and paper in a relatively short time.

Our first problem can be formulated mathematically right from the tables. From the first row we derive the following: $F1W1 + F1W2 + F1W3 + F1W4 = 600$. This equation states that the amount shipped from F1 to W1, plus the amount shipped from F1 to W2, plus the amount shipped from F1 to W3, plus the amount shipped from F1 to W4 must equal 600 units. In short, this means that the total amount shipped from factory one to all the warehouses must be equal to 600 units. This is a supply equation, and we can develop similar equations for the second, third, and fourth rows.

Continuing down the columns of the table, we can develop demand equations for the warehouses. Starting in the first column for W1, we derive the following: $F1W1 + F2W1 + F3W1 + F4W1 = 800$. This equation states that the sum of the factory shipments for each of the factories to warehouse W1 must be equal to 800 units. Similar equations are developed for the other columns.

These eight equations represent the mathematical model for the problem, and any solution to these will represent a feasible solution to the problem. With this set of equations we include an equation that represents the total cost. The object of linear programming, then, is to find the minimum total cost subject to the eight constraint equations. In this particular case the constraint equations constitute the four supply equations developed for the factories and the four demand equations for the warehouses.

13

Models and the Simplex Method

T$_{HIS}$ chapter covers a more sophisticated approach to linear programming—the simplex technique. After a brief explanation of the technique, the remainder of the chapter is devoted to models by way of practical examples. There are many types of linear programming problems that will not fit the transportation technique. These are "classical" types of problems, and they are far more abundant than transportation types. Classical problems lend themselves to the simplex technique of formulation and solution; in fact, all linear programming problems can be formulated and solved with the simplex technique. The reverse, however, cannot be said for the transportation technique.

The simplex technique moves from one solution to another by the algebraic manipulation of a set of linear equations. The equations constitute what is called the model. With simplex we move from one solution to another, improving the objective function with each step, until an optimum is reached. We are not interested in the detailed steps involved in manipulating the equations, because a proper explanation of these steps presumes a thorough working knowledge of linear algebra. Our focus is therefore on the model formulation.

We have said that the simplex model consists of a set of linear equations. Recall that some models are abstract, linear, and static—this fits perfectly the characteristics of a linear equation. Beyond this, however, what is a linear equation? One of the best definitions for our purpose is that it provides the coordinates of a map and it describes an object in space. An equation in two variables x and y describes a straight line in a rectangular or two-dimensional coordinate system. In Exhibit 13.1 we have drawn an object in two-dimensional space.

EXHIBIT 13.1

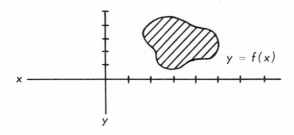

The equation $y = f(x)$ means that y is equal to some function of the variable x. Every equation has a graph, which in our figure is the shaded area in the rectangular coordinate system in x and y. We have arbitrarily drawn the graph, and we assume that we can formulate an equation in x to describe the graph. If we forget for just a moment all the algebra involved in equations and concentrate on the fact that every equation has a graph, we can begin to understand how equations can be used to represent working models.

The first step in linear programming is to define the alternatives; however, in many cases this is computationally impossible because the alternatives are infinite. Equations, on the other hand, can be used to *bound* all the alternatives. As an example, we can use the equation $y = f(x)$ in Exhibit 13.1 to bound all the possible alternatives in a business problem. Let's assume that a company manufactures two products x and y. We want to know how much of each we will produce in some forthcoming period. The quantity of x and y are not independent of each other, because certain of the resources used in the production of x are also used in the production of y—the more we produce of x the less we produce of y. The relationship between these two products can be expressed in the form of an equation. Let's assume that the equation is $y = f(x)$, as given in Exhibit 13.1. All points within the shaded area represent feasible alternatives. If we pick any point for x in the shaded area, we are restricted to only a certain set of points for y. We see here that equations can be of considerable help in defining all available alternatives. It would otherwise have been impossible to represent each alternative numerically because there are an infinite number of points. The problem of examining each of the points in the region will be dealt with later.

There are two equations in Exhibit 13.2: $y = g(x)$ and $y = h(x)$; g and h are some function of x, and g is not the same as h. Both equations have graphs that intersect in the shaded area. This shaded area is the place where both equations are true simultaneously. All points outside this area are points that (1) belong to neither $h(x)$ nor $g(x)$, (2) belong only to $g(x)$, or (3) belong only to $h(x)$. We see, then, how two equations restrict the area of alternatives even further.

EXHIBIT 13.2

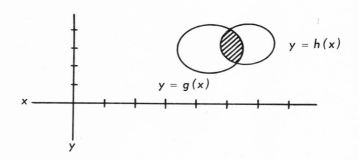

This case is similar to our first example, where we had one equation describing the production function for products x and y. If we add a second equation to that example—say, one that spells out a minimum amount of production for both x and y, we restrict the area of alternatives for that problem. Thus several equations work together to cut down the number of alternatives. In many linear programming problems there are literally hundreds of such equations, each representing some further restriction on the problem. Later we will see more specifically how these equations are formulated and how all the equations are straight lines and not circular as we have here in our examples.

There are several points that should be kept in mind. First, every equation has a graph that can be described in space. Second, several equations produce several graphs, and where these graphs intersect we have a common area that is bounded by the graphs. Third, in linear programming this area represents the area of feasible alternatives.

At this stage we must formulate a technique for assigning a single value to each point in the area and then finding the optimum value. We do this with another equation, called the objective function. It is similar in structure to the other equations in the model and, what's more important, has a graph that passes through the area of feasible solutions. The equation is formulated in such a way that every point in the region is assigned a single value, such as $y = j(x)$, where j is some function of x. The graph of this equation will help us to find the optimum point, because it will pass through all feasible solutions. We then need only to pick either the maximum or the minimum point on the graph of $y = j(x)$.

We are now in a position to formulate the general linear programming problem, given the following set of equations.

(1) $y = f(x)$
(2) $y = g(x)$
(3) $y = h(x)$
(4) $y = j(x)$

The first three equations describe some region in a graph; the fourth is the objective equation. We wish to optimize equation (4), subject to equations (1), (2), and (3). This means that we must find the maximum or minimum value for the objective equation, within the region described by the first three equations. Exhibit 13.3 should help clarify the problem.

EXHIBIT 13.3

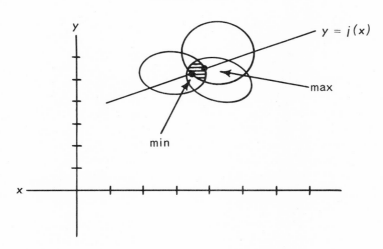

In the exhibit is a shaded area described by the graphs of equations (1), (2), and (3). We assume that the equations are somewhat circular objects with the common area which has been shaded in. The straight line that goes through the shaded region is the graph of equation (4) $y = j(x)$ which is called the objective function. We wish to find either the maximum or minimum point. These points are normally called extreme or optimum points. Remember, only those points on $y = j(x)$ which fall within the shaded region are eligible candidates. We can see that the maximum y point is reached where the line $y = j(x)$ just touches the edge of the shaded region at the highest value of y reading along the vertical y axis. This point is designated by an arrow labeled "max." The minimum point—below the maximum point relative to the vertical y axis—is where the line just touches the edge of the shaded region at the lowest point. The point is designated by an arrow labeled "min."

This description of a linear programming problem is an oversimplification, but at the same time it is not general enough. Yet most of us would bog down in the technical detail required for a complete description of a linear programming problem. The general formulation for the problem is—

1. To define feasible alternatives by formulating a set of equations that describe a graph in some space. The common area on the graph is the area of feasible alternatives.
2. To formulate a single equation, called the objective equation. This might represent total cost or total profit. This equation also has a graph that passes through the common area of the equations in point 1.
3. To pick either the maximum point, in the case of the total profit, or the minimum point, in the case of the total cost, on the objective graph within the common area described by point 1.

This is the crux of linear programming. The description is somewhat general and a bit oversimplified, but I think that if we understand the logic of this formulation, we know more about linear programming than we would if we followed a more orthodox line of reasoning.

We are now prepared to develop some practical models with our technique. Our first problem will be in the area of distribution of resources—specifically, in the area of machine assignment. Let us assume that a manufacturer has scheduled a given quantity of parts to be produced over a specified interval of time. He wants to produce these parts on available equipment at minimum cost.

There are three parts to be produced—P1, P2, and P3. The parts are to be produced on three machines—M1, M2, and M3—and each machine can produce each part. The only difference is that because of age and certain differences in automatic controls, the machines require varying amounts of time to complete a part. Some machines might require additional setup time at the beginning or might require an extra setup during the run. Older machines might require additional down time for scheduled preventive maintenance.

The time required for each machine to produce each part, and the costs associated with each activity, are shown in Exhibit 13.4. M1 takes 9.5 hours to produce one part P2, and M3 takes 5.4 hours to produce one part P1. Each machine has 160 hours of availability during the specific period. Requirements for parts are shown along the bottom row.

EXHIBIT 13.4

	P1	P2	P3	Maximum Availability
M1	A 19 4.1	B 38 9.5	C 75 12.3	160
M2	D 27 4.8	E 63 10.4	F 44 9.5	160
M3	G 24 5.4	H 58 11.4	I 48 8.7	160
Required Parts	50	20	30	

The costs associated with each activity are shown in the upper right-hand corner of each square; for example, it costs $63 to produce one part P2 on machine M2. The cost data are based on variable costs only. They include such items as operator rate on a parts basis, power consumption on a parts basis, scheduled and unscheduled down time on a per-part basis, and normal equipment depreciation on a per-part basis. The plant burden is not included in the cost figures because it does not belong there. Furthermore, in linear problems such as these this cost would cancel itself out because it occurs as a constant everywhere.

The manufacturer is now faced with the problem of deciding which parts are to be produced on which machines at a minimum total cost. In this problem let us arbitrarily label the squares in Exhibit 13.4. Starting with the square in the upper left-hand corner and moving to the right across the first row, assign A, B, C. Moving down one row and again starting from the left, assign D, E, F, and continuing to the third row, assign G, H, I. These letters represent the activities or variables to be resolved.

We can now formulate a mathematical model for this particular job.

Let us start by formulating a capacity constraint inequality for machine one. The constraint will limit use of M1 to less than 160 hours. Working directly across the first row of the table we get: (1) 4.1A + 9.5B + 12.3C $\leq$ 160. This is an inequality that constrains the use of machine M1 to fewer than 160 hours. In words, it says that the total time used on machine M1 is the sum of three components. The first component, 4.1A, represents the time consumed in making part P1; that is, the number of P1 made (A) times the amount of time required for each (4.1 hours). The second, 9.5B, represents the time consumed in making part P2; that is, the number of P2 made (B) times the amount of time required for each (9.5 hours). The third, 12.3C, represents the time consumed in making part P3—that is, the number of P3 made (C) times the amount of time required for each (12.3 hours). We can continue in this same fashion developing inequalities for machines M2 and M3 as follows: (2) 4.8D + 10.4E + 9.5F $\leq$ 160; (3) 5.4G + 11.4H + 8.7I $\leq$ 160.

Now we must develop production equations to meet the required demand. Working down the first column for part P1, we get: (4) A + D + G = 50. This equation insures that production of part P1 meets the required demand of 50 units. It says that P1 is the sum of three basic components: first, the number of P1 produced on M1 (A); second, the number of P1 produced on M2 (D); and third, the number of P1 produced on M3 (G). The following equations represent the production requirements for parts P2 and P3 respectively: (5) B + E + H = 20; (6) C + F + I = 30. Equations (4), (5), and (6) represent all the production requirements for this job. In the end they will insure that the required production levels are met.

Equations (1) through (6) represent the mathematical model for this particular job. Their common points represent the total feasible space— that is, all possible feasible alternatives. Any set of values for the variables that satisfies every equation will meet the job requirements. Conversely, any set of values that meets the job requirements will satisfy every equation.

The next step is to define the total cost from the variables. This can be taken directly from the cost table and is as follows: (7) 19A + 38B + 75C + 27D + 63E + 44F + 24G + 58H + 48I = Total Cost. This says that the total cost is equal to the sum of the number of parts produced by each process times its corresponding cost. The object of linear programming is to minimize the total cost (7) subject to the constraint equations (1) through (6), or find that solution to (1) through (6) which yields minimum total cost. This problem can now be solved by the simplex technique of linear programming.

Notice, however, that the actual technique must be conditioned to allow only integer, or whole number, solutions. It would make no sense to produce a fractional number of parts on a certain machine. We could allow for fractional answers and then make some final adjustments, but this would introduce the possibility of an answer that might not be quite the optimum.

Our second model will be for a problem in electric power distribution. A power company is faced with the problem of meeting a given power requirement for a specified period. Naturally, the company wishes to meet the requirements at minimum cost. The company has three generating plants that must supply power to three substations. The substations are strategically located within the area, and power is transferred from the plants to the substations as a block of power, after which it is divided and distributed throughout smaller regions.

Assume that for a given period the power requirements at each of the substations are known. The period in question depends upon management, but if it should be longer than 24 hours, the substation demand would have to reflect the maximum requirements during the day.

In this case, management decided that the period would be a four-hour interval and that demand at the substation would be the maximum required during this period. They reasoned that during a period of one day there was a complete shift in demand requirements from industrial to residential substations. Industrial area requirements were high during the day, and residential area requirements were high during the evening. Management therefore felt that the question of which generating plants were to fulfill the demand requirements at the substations to minimize operating cost should be considered in four-hour intervals, because there was a substantial shift in demand requirements for any interval beyond this.

In addition to this, it was obvious that demand requirements would vary substantially in the period of a week. Also, because demand requirements were generally increasing over a period of six months, management had to consider expansion in each of these periods. More important than this, it was experiencing a continuous shift in requirements throughout the area during these intervals. To keep costs down, it was forced to consider either building new generating plants closer to the load or increasing the efficiency of existing equipment with additional transformers and transmission lines of higher quality in an attempt to cut excessive power loss. A study of demand requirements over these periods was an essential first step in the attempt to cut operating costs.

To begin with, management decided to minimize operating costs in a four-hour period by finding the best assignment of generating plants to substations. The basic problem was to determine which generator should supply which substations, where each generating plant had a given capacity and each substation had a given demand. A closer look at this problem will show that it is quite similar to the transportation problem.

The table in Exhibit 13.5 shows the drop coefficients for each combination. For example, it takes 1.9 kilowatts of power at plant G2 to deliver 1.0 kilowatts of power to the load at substation S2. It takes 2.1 kilowatts of power at plant G3 to deliver 1.0 kilowatts of power to the load at substation S1.

EXHIBIT 13.5

	S1	S2	S3	Maximum Capacity (1,000 KW)
G1	A 19 1.3	B 19 2.0	C 19 1.8	40
G2	D 15 1.7	E 15 1.9	F 15 1.5	75
G3	G 17 2.1	H 17 1.1	I 17 1.9	65
Substation Demand (1,000 KW)	15	30	50	

The right-hand column shows the maximum capacity for each generating plant in thousands of kilowatts. Plant G2, for example, can produce no more than 75,000 kilowatts of power. The bottom row shows substation demand; that is, substation S2 requires 30,000 kilowatts of power.

Operating costs per thousand kilowatts produced are indicated in the upper right-hand corner of each square; for example, it costs $15 to produce and supply 1,000 kilowatts of power for 4 hours from plant G2 to any of the substations. Only the variable costs were considered. These include such items as operator rate, machine depreciation, fuel consumption, preventive maintenance, and so on, expressed in terms of 1,000 kilowatts of power produced. Costs that would have been incurred regardless of kilowatts produced were not included in the analysis.

From the data given in this exhibit we can develop a mathematical model of this particular job. Using the labeling procedure developed in the preceding section, we derive the following capacity constraint for generating plant G1: (1) $1.3A + 2.0B + 1.8C \leq 40$. The inequality says that the entire power output from generating plant G1 must be less than 40,000 kilowatts. The expression on the left of $\leq$ represents the output; on the right, the maximum capacity. The first term on the left, $1.3A$, represents the amount of power produced at G1 in order to deliver A units of power at substation S1.

We can develop a similar set of equations for the other generating plants, thus establishing all the capacity requirements. Production or demand equations can be developed from the columns of the table. For substation S1 we get: (2) $A + D + G = 15$. This equation insures that 15,000 kilowatts of power are supplied to substation S1.

Combining both the capacity constraints and the production constraints will give the mathematical model for the job. Any solution to this set will be a feasible solution to the problem. We can develop an expression for total cost directly from the cost table as follows: $19A + 19B + 19C + 15D + 15E + 15F + 17G + 17H + 17I =$ Total Cost. The objective is to minimize the total cost equation subject to the production and capacity constraints.

The model has other uses than determining the optimum allocation. In the final solution we may consider either making some improvements or closing down plants completely, transferring the production capability to a plant that has no idle capacity. We may consider opening a new plant. The model can also be used to study expansion. If we increase the capacity in the model at each of the plants by a fixed amount and then solve the problem for least cost, we may find that some plant is completely idle. This plant should be closed in the next expansion. We can also add plants to the model and solve it to determine where to locate new plants or determine what new equipment might be used.

Linear programming is a natural tool for the resolution of many types of linear blending problems, for both fluids and solids. It is being used extensively in the petroleum, steel, chemical, and paper industries for determining the optimum raw material mix to obtain an end product with specified characteristics at a minimum cost or at a maximum profit.

Assume that a manufacturer of household cleaning fluids has discovered a new cleaning fluid better than anything so far introduced on the market. He decides that the product's cost could be set at a level which, although somewhat higher than his current line, would be competitive. From initial estimates the costs appear to be on the border line between success and failure. The product has five basic ingredients in the following proportions:

Ingredient	*Required Percent of Final Mixture*
A	12
B	7
C	18
D	3
E	25
F [inert ingredients]	35

Initial cost estimates were based on procuring 100 percent solutions of each ingredient and blending them in the specified proportions. The cost of this approach was borderline, but other possible solutions were available to the manufacturer. He could procure raw materials, do his own refining, and develop 100 percent solutions of each ingredient. This approach, however, required a substantial investment in refining equipment.

Alternatively, he could procure certain semirefined solutions that contained variable proportions of one or more of the required ingredients, and then blend them in the correct proportions to obtain the required mix. This approach may or may not work depending on the availability and composition of the solutions themselves. Because the costs of these solutions were less than the costs of the 100 percent solutions, the product cost used would be substantially reduced if the right combination of solutions existed.

Even for ingredients which could not be procured as a blend of something else, the 100 percent solution could be used to meet the requirements of the final mixture. In this case four of the required ingredients could be met by blending less than 100 percent solutions, and the fifth could be met with a 100 percent solution. Since this approach to the problem would be cheaper than purchasing all five 100 percent solutions, it was considered the best answer.

Following a study of market availability, a table of supply (Exhibit 13.6) was compiled. Suppliers are shown across the top row of the table and the required ingredients are listed in the left-hand column. The figures within the table show the percentage of ingredient available in each supplier's solution; for example, supplier V's solution contains 5 percent of ingredient C and 31 percent of ingredient A. Suppliers Q, R, S, T, and U are the sources of the 100 percent solutions for each ingredient; for example, supplier R has a 100 percent solution of ingredient B.

The bottom row of the table gives the price per gallon of each supplier's solution, and the column on the right-hand side of the table shows the required percentage of each ingredient. The specifications require that the final solution contain at least the specified proportion; for example,

EXHIBIT 13.6

	Q	R	S	T	U	V	W	X	Y	Z	Required Percent
A	100					31	17	10	18		12
B		100					18		11	2	7
C			100			5		22		36	18
D				100		4	5		11		3
E					100	10	40			35	25
F						50	20	68	60	27	35
Price Per Gallon	1.9	2.8	2.3	2.1	1.5	1.0	1.7	1.1	1.0	.9	

the final solution must contain at least 7 percent of ingredient B. Inert ingredients—labeled F in the table—must not exceed 35 percent of the final solution.

We start developing the model by formulating an equation that insures that one gallon of the final solution is made. This equation, a computational convenience, is as follows: (1) $Q + R + S + T + U + V + W + X + Y + Z = 1.0$. The equation says that the sum of solutions supplied from all suppliers must be equal to one gallon.

From the first row of the table we can develop the following inequality which will insure that ingredient A will meet the specified proportion in the final solution: (2) $Q + .31V + .17W + .10X + .18Y \geq .12$. The inequality says that the sum of the quantities provided by each supplier times its corresponding percentage must be at least as large as .12 in the final solution. For example, if supplier X is contributing .25 gallons and suppliers Q, V, and W are contributing nothing, supplier Y must contribute at least .53 gallons to the final mixture in order for (2) to be true.

We can add to (2) a slack variable that will indicate the excess of ingredient A in the final solution and thereby make an equation from (2) as

Quantitative Business Planning Techniques   165

follows: (3) $Q + .31V + .17W + .10X + .18Y - SA = .12$. The variable SA will give the amount of excess in ingredient A. If, for instance, suppliers Q, V, and W contribute nothing, X contributes .25 gallons, and Y contributes .75 gallons, then the excess of A in the final mixture is $SA = .04$, or 4 percent. We continue to establish similar equations for the other ingredients.

For F, the inert ingredients, the inequality is less than .35. It is written as follows: (4) $.5V + .2W + .68X + .6Y + .27Z \leq .35$. Since suppliers V, W, X, Y, and Z are the only contributors to the inert portion of the ingredient, they are the only ones represented in equation (4). The coefficients on the variables come from the row labeled F in the table. Remember that the inert ingredients may not exceed 35 percent of the final solution; hence the inequality is stipulated by $\leq$. Adding a positive slack variable to this inequality transforms it into an equation. The slack variable will indicate the difference between the actual amount of inert ingredients in the final solution and 35 percent.

Combining all equations, we can derive the mathematical model for this job, and the set will define all the feasible alternatives for the job. Any set of solutions to the model is a feasible solution for the problem. The intersection of all the equations in the model defines an area in a 16-dimensional space—that is, there are 16 variables in the model. The area in this space has an infinite number of points in it because there are fewer equations than variables. Each point in the area has 16 coordinates associated with it and every point in the space will satisfy every equation.

We develop an expression for total cost from the bottom row of the table as follows: $1.9Q + 2.8R + 2.3S + 2.1T + 1.5U + 1.0V + 1.7W + 1.1X + 1.0Y + .9Z = \text{Total Cost}$. This equation says that the total cost for the final mixture is equal to the sum of the price per gallon times the number of gallons from each supplier. The equation transforms each point in the area defined by the model into a single value—total cost. The object of linear programming is to find the solution to the model that produces a minimum value solution to the total cost equation.

14

Linear Programming Applied to the Computer

This chapter covers the development of the systems design that will enable us to implement a linear programming system on a digital computer. We are interested here not in the mathematics of linear programming but only in how we can use the technique on a computer. We also want to consider how best to set up a problem and how we should interface with the computer. In what ways do we want to enter data into the system, and in what ways do we want data to come out of the system?

Finally, after we have pinned down these more general details we will want to decide what hardware should be considered to accomplish the objectives. Notice that this we do last, not first. This seems reasonable. But, contrary to what appears reasonable, most companies buy or rent computer hardware before they have thoroughly considered the applications to be accomplished. In this chapter we will *not* follow the lead of the majority of industry.

Let's begin with a general description of what we want the system to do. The system will accept input data describing some model in the real world, manipulate the data using the simplex or revised simplex technique, and determine the optimum solution (if there is any solution at all and if the problem has a finite optimum solution).

Following this general formulation of system objectives, it is appropriate to itemize more specifically each of the basic system objectives.

1. The system must accept input data in the form of either magnetic tape or punch cards. This input data will consist of two parts:

    a. *Control information,* which will be entered in the form of commands telling the system what to do and what to expect next.

    b. *Numerical information,* which describes the specific problem. There will actually be three pieces of information describing each coefficient that is entered into the system. This information will name the numerical quantity itself and identify both the row and the column within the problem where the coefficient belongs. Only nonzero coefficients need to be entered into the system; all other coefficients will be assumed to be at zero.

The format on the cards will be the same as the format on magnetic tape; there will be 80 columns of information. Exactly which columns contain which information can be described in a detailed design specification.

2. The system will load the problem information, packing all nonzero information on mass storage devices, and it will sort the information into the proper rows and columns.

3. The system will consist mainly of MACRO commands, which allow the user to control the system and tailor each job to the specific requirements.

4. It will maintain, and update as required, a library of MACRO commands. The library will contain the names of user-defined MACRO commands along with the basic system MACROs. This will give the user the opportunity to make up his own commands from existing commands.

5. It will contain an arithmetic algorithm, which is equivalent to either the simplex or the revised simplex technique. This algorithm will start with any solution and proceed automatically from one iteration to the next, improving the objective function with each step until an optimum has been reached if possible. During each iteration the program will examine a manual switch to see whether operator intervention is required. If it is, the program will move the entire image of the problem to mass storage and set all necessary parameters, so that the problem can be restarted from that point at a later time.

6. The system will have the capability to solve a problem in either single- or double-precision arithmetic.

7. It will contain a subprogram that will reduce rounding errors to a minimum.

8. It will maintain two sets of problem data. One set will consist of the

13. LBRY tells the system that a string of commands follows. This string of commands is to be entered into the library under a new command name, which the system will find on the first card following this one. Whenever this new command name is encountered in the job stream, the system will go to the library and replace the name with the string of commands found there.

14. CHG causes the system to change the values of certain coefficients in the original problem. Cards following specify the row, column, and new value of the coefficient.

15. ERRORS causes the system to take the final solution values for the variables that remain in the optimum solution and plug them into the original problem as it was initially loaded to see how much error results. These results are to be printed out for comparison between what should have resulted and what actually resulted.

16. RESTART causes the system to restart the solution algorithm on a problem that is currently half-solved. The problem will be stored in a pre-specified format on disc or drum.

These minimum commands are necessary in order to run a linear programming problem. No major linear programming system in existence today is without these commands; in fact, the Univac, IBM, GE, CDC, and SDS scientific systems have at least three times as many. If we intend to use linear programming, we must learn these commands in order to interface with the system.

In the preceding chapter we developed a problem in blending. In this situation, we found that the inventor defined a set of required ingredient specifications for ingredients A through F. These were expressed as a percentage of the final mixture. We also had several alternative vendors. Vendors Q through U supplied 100 percent refined solutions of each of the ingredients. Other vendors sold unrefined solutions that had portions of the required ingredients but in the wrong percentages. The problem was to find the right combination of vendors to meet the required specifications at minimum cost.

We derived a model for this problem on the basis of the data from Exhibit 13.6. Now we want to set up this problem for the computer, using the specified commands. The sequence of punch cards in Exhibit 14.1 is fairly representative of how we would set up the problem for the computer.

The 17 commands shown in the exhibit are all that are needed to solve the problem. We start off at command 1, the LOAD command, which is followed by the cards containing the coefficients from the table in Exhibit 13.6. Each of these cards contains the row name, the column name, and the actual value of the coefficient. In this case, we label row 1 the A

EXHIBIT 14.1

1. LOAD

A	Q	1.0
B	R	1.0
C	S	1.0
D	T	1.0
E	U	1.0
A	V	.31
C	V	.05
D	V	.04
E	V	.1
F	V	.5
A	W	.17
.		
.		
.		
PRICE	Q	1.9
PRICE	R	2.8
.	.	.
.	.	.
PRICE	Z	.9

A	PRCNT	.12
B	PRCNT	.07
C	PRCNT	.18
.		
.		
F	PRCNT	.35

2. MIN   PRICE
3. SP
4. SET   SCREEN   .00001
5. OPTM
6. PRNT

    PRICE
    PRCNT
    PRICE   PRCNT

7. SET

    TEMP TO PRICE   PRCNT

8. INVRT
9. OPTM
10. SET

    NEW TO PRICE   PRCNT

11. IF

    TEMP − NEW < .01   15

12. DP
13. INVRT
14. OPTM
15. PRNT

    PRICE
    PRCNT
    PRICE   PRCNT

16. ERRORS
17. END

row and column 1 the Q column. The bottom row, which is the objective function, is labeled PRICE. The right-hand side, or the percent column, is labeled PRCNT. Notice that the price and percentage data are entered as regular problem variables.

Command 2 tells the system that it is to minimize the problem and that the objective function is the row labeled PRICE. Command 3 sets the system to work in single-precision arithmetic. Command 4 sets the value SCREEN to .00001. SCREEN is a location in parameter storage and is used as a screening constant. Any value in the system which becomes smaller than this value is rounded to zero. Values smaller than this may cause rounding problems that would make the system cycle indefinitely.

Command 5 directs the system to optimize the problem that was previously loaded into the system. The system employs some version of the simplex algorithm at this point and, through a series of iterations, continuously moves variables into the solution, which makes the PRICE row smaller with each iteration. When no more improvements can be made in the PRICE row, the OPTM command is complete and the system returns to the main control routine. At this point, the system should have reached what, numerically at least, appears to be a minimum solution to the problem.

Command 6 directs the system to print out three things. First, the PRICE row is printed out. These values are constant; they have not changed since they were loaded into the system. However, we decide to have them printed out as a convenience at this point. Second, the PRCNT column is printed out. This gives us the final solution by printing out the extreme right-hand column of the current solution, with each variable along with its value. Third, a single value, which is from the PRICE row in the PRCNT column, is printed out to give us the total cost of the final solution.

Command 7 sets the value TEMP to the total cost, and command 8 goes back to the start and proceeds directly to the answers that we had at the end of command 5. This helps minimize the rounding errors. Command 9 attempts to reoptimize the problem, to see whether eliminating rounding errors changed the final solution, and command 10 sets the value named NEW to equal the total cost of the new solution arrived at in command 9.

Command 11 is a branch command that specifies a condition to be checked. In this case, the system is to see whether the difference between the old and new total cost is less than .01. If so, it goes to command 15; if not, it proceeds to command 12. If the system arrives at command 12, we know that there were significant rounding errors between commands 5 and 9; therefore, we should try a third solution in double precision. At command 12 the system sets itself in a double-precision mode. At command 13 it reinverts the problem, and at command 14 it reoptimizes the problem.

If the program moves to command 15, there is nothing more that can be done to minimize rounding errors so it prints out the data. Command 16 executes an error analysis that tells us how reliable our answers are, and command 17 ENDs the run.

If we examine various linear programming systems, we'll find that this is a fairly representative example. We can see that the computer handles the mathematics of the problem; our main job is to set up the problem and understand the command language. This completes most of our system requirements; now we can determine what hardware is required to implement such a system.

To begin with, we need a computer with floating point arithmetic. This usually means that the memory word size must be at least 32 bits, which is almost useless for big problems. As for the required core memory, we will take all we can get if we are interested only in speed. Typically, the program is set up to work on subsets of the problem, which reside in the core memory. The larger the subset, the faster the system.

The total problem resides on disc or drum, and the system is designed to pick as many columns of the problem as it can get into memory at one time. When the program completes one set of columns, it goes back to disc to get some more. As an example, if a problem has 400 rows and 1,000 columns, the core requirement for the fastest possible solution is 400,000 locations. This is, of course, out of the question because 32,000 locations is the average for a system, and the program itself takes almost 20,000 locations. This leaves room for only 12,000 locations of core working space. If we use double precision, this figure will be cut in half to 6,000 locations. Because we must work with not less than a whole column at a time in linear programming, the best we can possibly do is to work on 30 columns at a time. This is roughly what happens in most good linear programming systems.

It is therefore desirable to have a fast drum or disc to back up the system's memory shortage. In the end, the speed of this device will indirectly determine the running time of the problem. Usually, the internal speed of the computer is such that it will stay far ahead of the input and output capabilities of the disc or drum.

In our situation of a 1,000-column problem, there are 1,000 references to the disc or drum for each pass through all the columns. It would take roughly 3,000 references to complete one basic iteration. One iteration in the case of a 400-row problem with 12,000 memory locations would produce up to 30 new variables. This means that, starting from the beginning, we would need to change at least 400 of the variables, but realistically, it would end up closer to 1,200 changes. By dividing 30 into 1,200, we get 40 iterations as the average for a problem with 400 rows and 1,000 columns. In terms of drums or disc references, this would mean 40 times 3,000, or 120,000 references. Each reference on a disc takes an average of 20 milliseconds, or 20 thousandths of a second. If we multiply the time by the number of references, we get a total running time of 2,400 seconds, or 40 minutes.

It is difficult to better this speed, no matter what the capabilities of the central computer, without reducing the access time to the drum or disc. There *is* a way to improve the speed without changing the mass storage access time—by buying another 12,000 memory locations. If we do this we can work on 60 columns at a time, thereby requiring only 20 iterations, which would cut the running time in half.

On the disc or drum, whichever we choose, we need room for at least the following:

1. 100,000 locations to contain the original problem.
2. 100,000 locations to contain the dynamic problem as it changes from one iteration to the next.
3. 50,000 locations for the library.
4. 10,000 locations to contain an index of symbolic names with numerical names for rows and columns.
5. 32,000 locations for an image dump of core memory.
6. 100,000 locations to contain those segments of the program that currently are not in use and therefore need not always occupy main memory.
7. 100,000 locations for working scratch space.

This means we need at least 500,000 mass storage locations to run the problem.

The mass storage device and the central computer constitute the key critical hardware components for a good linear programming system. Some systems use tape, but these usually run too slowly to solve a larger problem. Many manufacturers will supply a package which is three times as extensive as the one we have developed here and, in most cases, unnecessarily sophisticated. But in all cases they have built the system around a drum or disc. In addition to mass storage, we need a card reader for the initial loading of the problem and a printer for printing out the results. If we want to do partial runs that require dumping and reloading at a future time, we also need magnetic tape.

Although many practical applications for linear programming have been mentioned, caution should be the watchword. These problems are all classical examples, and often the slightest variation puts the problem completely out of the realm of linear programming. Do not be convinced too quickly that all problems which present alternatives can be optimized with linear programming. Chances are that they cannot. Probably only a small percentage, if any at all, will fall within the reach of this technique. But linear programming is a growing science, and what is true today may not be true next year. If the science continues to grow at the current rate, at least twice as many applications will exist five years from now. Clearly, every company of any size should be exploring potential applications for linear programming even if none exist today. Chances are that the effort will pay for itself within a short period. However, applications rather than theory should be emphasized—the theory can be left to the mathematicians.